"SCREENWRITING 001"

By

Hafed Bouassida, Ph.D.

Mediterraneo Publishing

2014

Published

By

Mediterraneo Publishing

7723 Pondwood Drive
Edina, MN 55439

952-818-6428

Mediterraneo001@yahoo.com

Cover Design

By

Jeremy Bandow

Printed

By LuLu.com

Copyright © 2014 by Hafed Bouassida

**Library of Congress
Cataloging-in-Publication Data**

ISBN-13: 978-0-9893269-2-6

"To make a great movie, you need just three things:
A great script, a great script, and a great script."

Alfred Hitchcock
Director

THE CONTENT

CHAPTER ONE

IN LIEU OF AN INTRODUCTION

"Becoming a writer is not a career decision, like becoming a doctor or a policeman. You don't choose it so much as you get chosen, and once you accept the fact that you are not fit for anything else, you have to be prepared to walk a long, hard road for the rest of your days."

Paul Auster
Screenwriter, Director
Smoke

So you've decided to become a screenwriter.

A wise, honorable and laudable decision!

After all, who could better tell the adventures of your Uncle Abernathy, the black sheep of the family? Bernie as he likes to be called, procrastinated his life in the Virgin Islands, never agreed to marry, joined a religious order on a tiny forgotten island at 65, for one year, then eloped with a young nun from a nearby convent, married her and both became the owners of the most exclusive bordello in the Caribbean…

What about that neighbor of yours, that disgustingly beautiful and alluring widow who is getting married next week for the fifth time? All her exes mysteriously died... Sure, the police investigated as long as they could. Nothing, zilch, nada! Heck, there must be a story there, particularly when the next husband in line happens to be Georges Clooney, with whom you happen to be madly in love!

Which reminds me of Williston and Delilah, madly in love since my high school days, and both still mad about each other; they have married and divorced each other about half a dozen times, robbed banks together, went to jail together and freed each other several times from jails in the most spectacular ways: explosions, chases, helicopters, abductions, the whole gamut! Today, both close to sixty and both in high security jails, they are seeking the review of their case by the Supreme Court of United States: The jail authorities have refused them the right to get married under the Constitution for the seventh time…

*And how about that persistent dream of yours? The one where you fly like **Superman**, and you just saved the life of that drop-dead gorgeous Brazilian model from **Victoria's Secret**, whatever her name is. But your current girlfriend, who happens to be **Jennifer Lawrence, Scarlett Johansson, Charlize Theron** or whatever babe you dream of, does not appreciate your powers. They end up fighting over you, until **Brad Pitt** shows up with **Angelina Jolie**, and they get you to adopt five kids from Africa. And there you go, flying with your entire family, the drop-dead gorgeous Brazilian model, your own favorite babe, five adopted kids, Brad Pitt and Angelina Jolie, all in Superman costumes, helping the poor and the destitute!*

Note to my students and to all inadvertent readers:
*Don't even try to steal any of these ideas or develop them
into scripts. First, they stink! Second, they are awfully
childish; Third, I definitely own them, so I am in control;
fourth, I am developing them.*

So, just don't try anything!

Back to your decision to become a screenwriter!

*The point is, any of these stories of yours can trump
pompous movies such as **Magnolia, Independence Day, Titanic,**
or that insipid and confusing **Memento,** not to mention the
insane **Adaptation** or **Eternal Sunshine of the Spotless Mind.**
If they can get away with such inanities, why not you? If
someone such as **Shane Black** was able to get his first
script, **Lethal Weapon,** transformed into a blockbuster, why
not you? I mean is **Quentin Tarantino** - who was just a video
store clerk, never went to school and never wrote a script-
such a genius for writing **Reservoir Dogs** or **Pulp Fiction?**
What's with some guys ranting philosophical essays before
stomping a few bad boys?*

Then, there is the money and the fame.

***Shane Black** of **Lethal Weapon** fame was paid close to
two million for his subsequent screenplays; **Joe Esterhaz**
who fomented that sex-filled thriller **Basic Instinct,**
pulled three million! And what about the likes of **William
Goldman** or **Robert Towne** who are paid more than one million
just to help rewrite scripts that are not even theirs?*

*And even if you don't happen to be part of the
screenwriters' pantheon, the minimum paid for an original
script today runs close to a $120,000. Conservatively,
that's $1,000 a page! Not bad for a page that's not even
filled with words.*

*Finally, some famous screenwriters have become
household names, close to earning a star status! Many of
them have been able to move up the ladder and become
directors, producers or executive producers of their next
movies, with all the fame and money that such positions
bring.*

*So, all things considered, deciding to become a
screenwriter does not seem to be such a bad idea,
particularly given your undeniable talent with words.*

You definitely have a chance!

But there are just a few problems with this decision.

The very day you decided to become a screenwriter, between forty and fifty scripts were submitted to every story department in every studio and network in Hollywood.

Between three and ten scripts were submitted to every respectable independent production company in New York and Los Angeles.

Hundred to hundred and fifty scripts were registered through the **Writers Guild of America (WGA).**

I don't have the numbers for scripts that were registered directly with the Copyright Office, but it is safe to imagine the same number as with the WGA, which means another hundred to hundred and fifity scripts.

And I am not counting the scripts that are already in development in different studios, the ones that are slated for coverage, and the ones that are in the meanders of the dizzying turn-around. That number is between 50 and 100 at any given time in every single studio.

I am also not counting the hundreds of scripts that enter daily in contests, competitions and grants of all kinds. That very day you made your decision, twenty scripts were entered in the famous **Nicholl Fellowship** *in L.A., ten into the* **Sundance Lab,** *the* **Austin SXSW** *or the N.Y.* **Tribeca** *and at least one was entered in one of Minneapolis major contests or grant organizations:* **McKnight, Bush, and Jerome Foundations.**

All that for a mere four to five hundred total produced movies per year in the US…

Not very good odds: If my mathematical skills are still intact, for every thousand submitted scripts, 800 are flatly rejected, 100 maybe are covered, 20 are developed, probably five are green-lighted, two end up being produced and only one is finally distributed in theaters! Sobering, as it were…

There is more: Of the 11,000 members of the Writers Guild of America:

About a third are retired or "emeritus" at any given time.

Less than half of the remaining members, around 3,000, had any work last year in L.A., the Mecca of filmmaking.

Of those, only 1,500 reported any income from feature films.

20% among them made less than $4,000.

Only 10% made more than $7,000.

The median earning of the WGA working members was close to $75,000. Looks tempting, but that's an average, obviously misleading, as it combines the amazing million dollar incomes of the very few and the zero-dollar basic incomes of the very many.

Sorry to do this, there is even more in Tinsel Town:

Only 25% of the writers over 40 get any writing assignment.

That percentage decreases to 15% if you happen to be over 50.

Hollywood considers you a dead writer by the time you reach 60.

Women and minorities account for less than 25% of all writing assignments, and that's a huge improvement over the preceding decade!

And they are paid less anyway, despite all federal and state efforts and laws: 10 to 25% less.

Now if you happen to be a woman, from a minority and over 60, you are screwed… and you obviously need a miracle!

New York and the rest of the country show even more alarming numbers.

So, you've decided to become a screenwriter.

A wise, honorable and laudable decision!

Despite the tough odds and all the preceding warnings, I hope you stick to your decision.

Just like the 3,500 Screenwriting students who join the UCLA Extension Writers Program every year!

Just like the many thousands who apply to the countless writing programs throughout the US.

Just like the more than one hundred students who join our MCTC screenwriting program every year.

They all hope to properly learn the ropes, the craft and maybe the art of writing for the screen.

They all hope to increase their odds, better their chance at entering the most competitive market in the world.

They all hope that in doing so, they have a better chance at writing their unique stories, and who knows, maybe if talented enough, become the next multimillion-dollar screenwriter…

After all, where would we be without ambition? Stick to your decision, but learn!

*And take to heart the wise words of **Linda Stuart**, a Hollywood story analyst: **"No one can teach writing talent. But you can learn craft, and that's what will save you at the end. Because once you learn the fundamental tools of the trade (plot progression, act structure, character, dialogue, and all the rest of it,) it will greatly reduce the margin for error and lead you to make far better choices. You won't settle for the same inadequacies over and over again when you didn't know any better. And when it comes time for someone to evaluate your work, whether it be a writing sample or a script for possible sale, you'll be ahead of the game."***

Now that you are aware of the consequences of your choices, here is my personal warning, so that we are all on the same page:

I do not like books,
I do not trust books,
I do not believe in books!

There you have it, the cat is out of the bag.

Don't get me wrong: Like most anybody else, I love a good book. I love to immerse myself in the world of a book that can transport me to places and spaces and times I have never been and where I will never go.

I grew up in a time when reading was a fundamental part of your education.

I grew up in a time when reading less than one book a day was considered a deficiency for which you needed to see a specialist.

I grew up in a time when reading was all you could afford. Our bulky TV set was securely locked and my father would let us watch cartoons and scientific documentaries once in a while, that is, if we behaved well.

So…

*Here is what I don't really like: the **How To** books that tout the amazing pretense to teach you music, or painting, or writing, or poetry, or screenwriting. Imagine **Music for Dummies**, or **Screenwriting for Dummies** or even **Poetry for Dummies**. Believe it or not, I have seen those!*

Let's agree on one basic principle I still hold central to my teaching: nobody can teach arts, period!

I consider myself a mentor, and my students are my disciples. And that's when I am on my best days. Otherwise, I am a simple craftsman trying to pass on some basic knowledge to my apprentices, hoping that maybe some of them, with enough talent and the will to explore it, will excel creatively and become real artists.

I can't remember ever promising to teach anyone the Art of Screenwriting. However, I did and I still do promise to help them learn the technique, the craft and the trade. But I can't guarantee anything beyond that, if there is no talent to start with.

Mastering the art is a two-way process, a two-way journey and quest that might or might not happen, even if you were to work like a slave for your entire life! If you bring some talent to the table, even a speck of it, there is a chance that you will succeed with a lot of hard work.

Now if you could bring a lot of it, things will definitely be easier. But if you bring nothing, no teacher will make an artist out of you, no matter what amount of work and dedication you will bring along. It's just hard to make anything out of nothing…

*Think about those two fundamentally opposed musicians: **Salieri,** the hard worker with very little talent, and **Mozart,** the amazingly talented artist who needed almost no effort to create, but who was lazy and unpredictable!*

That's why any book pretending to teach you the art of… whatever, is a lie and we have unfortunately become accustomed to accepting it at face value.

That's why this is not a book about the art of screenwriting or how to become an artist-screenwriter.

This is rather a textbook that aims to help you find the simple answers to the fundamental principles and basic rules that govern the craft of writing for the screen.

This is a technical manual to navigate through the maze of countless situations screenwriters could find themselves in, with the uncertainty of an artist who has no time for the rules.

This is a manual, a dictionary of sorts that students can use whenever in need or in doubt.

As you see, nowhere am I talking about the art. That might happen much later, after you have mastered the rules and principles, the technique, the craft. It might happen despite you and me, somewhere between the classroom, our personal endeavors and your subsequent regular writing.

And it's a miracle every time that happens!

CHAPTER TWO

PUTTING YOUR IDEAS ON THE PAGE

*"It is absolutely essential to learn the craft.
A producer wants to work with a writer who already knows
the general rules of what a screenplay should be.
But the difference between becoming a good and a great
writer depends on learning the craft,
then having the talent to take it a step above."*

Mace Neufeld
Producer
No Way Out
The Hunt for Red October

1/ *Page Setting*

What we write, the ideas we express and the emotions we hope to generate are actually as important as how we put our words on the page. How many lines, what's capitalized, what margins, what spacing, how long, how many words, etc., have become essential in the screenwriting process.

Lynda La Plante, the writer of **Prime Suspect** and **She's Out,** stresses that importance in simple terms: *"Get hold of a professionally formatted script and note everything; from simple instructions like INT. and EXT. to the exact length, and never stray from that format. You might submit a masterpiece but if it's not properly laid out, the reader may give up after scene one."*

Through the years, a set of rules has slowly emerged within the screenwriting community to precisely define how words are put on the pages of a script. Some call these rules **Format,** others **Master Scene Format** or **Script Format.**

Whatever the name, it makes sense for the filmmaking industry to agree on one single format with specific rules and principles, so that we all read and understand the same exact picture or dialogue, happening in the same exact way and lasting the same exact amount of time on screen. After all, it's all about that screen isn't it? You are writing for the screen, not for a novel or a play.

Linda Stuart, another Story Analyst, is unequivocal: *"If you are not familiar with script form, take the time to learn it! It matters! […] People who read scripts day in and day out respond best to what is collectively viewed as proper screenplay form."*

Imagine the following action:

===

Sarah slowly wanders through the promenade, her eyes blurred with tears. An epitome of sadness.

===

How long would that last on screen? In other words: How long do I see Sarah walking and crying?

For me as a reader, it could be five or six seconds, maybe ten. But for you as a writer, you might have in mind a whole minute of a gut-wrenching walk with Sarah crying her eyes out.

In terms of emotional response, the result is going to be different if the viewer is subjected to watching the poor gal crying her soul out for that long!

The fundamental question ultimately is: How do I know as a reader what was in your mind?

Imagine a director reading a script and understanding it in a completely different way than a writer, a producer, the actors, the production designer or the musician…

A writer should appropriately inform the reader, any reader, about a particular action and how long it will last on screen without the risk of misinterpretation. And every reader should more or less read the same, understand the same and hopefully feel emotionally the same.

That's why we need to all agree on a specific way of writing a script and understanding it.

That's why format, page setting and how we put words on the page are so important.

2/ Margins

*The fundamental principle in screenwriting is to avoid including many directions in your page. **Norm Saulnier,** a **Paramount** Story Analyst, wisely cautions: **"Don't try to cram huge amounts of descriptions on a page just so the script doesn't run over 120. Because if those 120 pages – printed normally would have been 145, it's too long."***

Here is how a normal script page should look:

*Left Margin: **1.5 in.***
*Right Margin: **1.25 in.***
*Top Margin: **1 in.***
*Bottom Margin: **1.00 to 1.25 in.***

But this requirement has luckily become largely mute as screenwriting software programs have decreased in price in the last few years: between $100 and $150, a one-time life investment! Smartly designed, these software programs will automatically provide you with the right setting and guide you through the arcane screenwriting principles.

Movie Magic Screenwriter and **Final Draft** are the most widely used software programs in the industry. Just use any of them, forget about your page setting and focus rather on the quality of your writing!

3/ Fonts

Definitely, the entire industry, all professionals, anyone who has the slightest hope to be even read, will have to use one agreed upon font: **12-point Courier!**

And there is a good reason for that: the screenplay format was developed during the typewriter era, and most screenplays until the beginning of the nineties were actually written on old typewriters (think **"Remington"** and other **"Royals"**), which used the traditional 12-point Courier font.

Particularly with the advent of new screenwriting software programs, new fonts have been developed, such as **Courier New, Courier Movie Magic Screenwriter,** or **Courier Final Draft.** In principle, all of these fonts are acceptable, provided they have the word Courier in their denomination and you can print them in 12-point.

However, slight differences can arise with the page count. Because of the default line spacing between the regular Courier and the Courier New font developed during the computer era, going from a hundred-page traditional Courier script to Courier New will increase your page count to 113 pages or more, depending on the page breaks. The fact is, Courier New puts a little more space between the lines.

The leading screenwriting software programs, wary of this dangerous difference that makes your script swell in terms of pages when using the Courier New, came up with ingenious new fonts: **Courier Movie Magic Screenwriter,** and **Courier Final Draft.** They allow for a slight adjustment of *the line spacing so that the page count stays close to the traditional Courier font. They even offer **Tight**, **Very Tight** or **Cheat** choices, which can bring the lines even tighter and the space between the words a little smaller. This is obviously used by screenwriters who are struggling to get their scripts from the unacceptable length of above 120 pages to the professional 118 or 119 pages.*

*Here is an example with the traditional **Courier** font:*

```
================================================================

Sarah slowly wanders through the promenade, her eyes
blurred with tears. An epitome of sadness.

================================================================
```

*And here is the same with the **Courier New** font:*

```
================================================================

Sarah slowly wanders through the promenade, her eyes
blurred with tears. An epitome of sadness.

================================================================
```

To the naked eye, the font and the space between the lines seem smaller, but in the final count, both will end up giving you more script pages.

*Here is now the same excerpt with a **Courier Movie Magic Screenwriter** font:*

```
================================================================

Sarah slowly wanders through the promenade, her eyes
blurred with tears. An epitome of sadness.

================================================================
```

As you can see, the Movie Magic Screenwriter Courier is pretty darn close to the traditional Courier.

*All things considered, I suggest that you stick with the **traditional Courier, the Screenwriter MM Courier,** or the **Final Draft Courier.** You would want to avoid Courier New as much as possible.*

*Finally, a script should be written using only these fonts, and this size, and **only on one side** of your page, including your cover page!*

Again, whichever software program you use will take care of the font and the size as well, provided that you use the right one.

4/ Spacing

*Both dialogue and directions are **single-spaced.** Anything else needs **double-spacing:** between paragraphs, consecutive dialogues, a dialogue and a direction or a direction and a dialogue.*

*Between scenes, we prefer **triple-spaces.** It makes for a better reading, as readers love to see empty space on a page. However, it makes for longer scripts too!*

So, faced with this dilemma, most screenwriters traditionally start by using triple-spaces. If the script goes beyond the magic 120 pages, they reformat it using double-spaces between scenes, thus trying to squeeze more pages into their scripts.

I know, it's a sort of cheat… but still acceptable!

Here is how it ends up:

```
================================================================

Richard hastily packs his files into a shabby attaché-case,
trying to avoid a direct confrontation with Jennifer.

                    RICHARD
                  (Angrily)
          Please, try to understand me--
```

                    JENNIFER
       I don't want to talk about it.
       Just leave me alone!

Overwhelmed with tears, Jennifer quickly walks out of the kitchen, SLAMMING the door behind her.

Richard STOPS his packing, surprised.

EXT. HENNEPIN AVENUE — AFTERNOON

Jennifer, still in tears, walks aimlessly through the afternoon crowd. Zombies leaving their boring jobs, rushing back into their monotonous lives… She bumps into some of them without even realizing their existence.

===

5/ Style

This is definitely the least of your problems; in screenwriting, it's a very straightforward issue:

We **DO NOT:**

> *Boldface!*
> *Italicize!*
> *Underline!*
> *Strikethrough,*
> *Outline,*
> *Superscript,*
> *Shadow,*
> *Engrave,*
> *Include Happy Faces,*
> *Use Arrows,*
> *Insert Marginalia to explain something to the reader,*

Or anything else your wild imagination might come up with! Nada! Zilch! Zero! Even for effect, neither in dialogue nor in descriptions!

Actually, doing so, you will reach one sure effect: being perceived as an amateur! **Michael Serafin** *thinks that:*

"…If a script comes in with even the tiniest drawing on it, we're probably looking at a neophyte."

6/ Page Numbers

Page numbers are indicated in the upper right-hand corner of the page, followed by a single period. And by the way, **DO NOT** ever number the first page! No one has a real clue why. Definitely another Hollywood quirk that has to do with superstition…

Here is how it should look:

```
================================================================

                                                        15.


INT. ANDERSON'S KITCHEN - DUSK


================================================================
```

7/ Directions/Descriptions/Stage Directions:

Directions, **Stage Directions** or **Descriptions** are information describing a setting, a location, a situation, a character, an action, a sound effect, an ambiance, etc. They are used to help you convey the events of your story, present your characters, describe their actions and reactions, and generally set up the mood of your narration.

Description is definitely the most essential part of your screenplay. It probably constitutes 70% to 80% of your entire script; the other 20 to 25% is your dialogue!

Yes, descriptions are that important! They describe an action and they convey the visuals, which from time to time might be two people talking. But that should never be the rule as movies have never been about dialogue… Theater on the other hand is all about dialogue!

Descriptions truly make all the difference in the world between a script written by a talented screenwriter, and one that's quickly half-baked by a dilettante who thinks that scripts are simply a bunch of dialogue put on a page!

Beside the rules presented in the paragraph about style (# 5), here are the few rules you need to remember when you put your directions on the page:

***Start** your descriptions at the agreed left margin and continue until you reach the right one.*

***DO NOT** ever justify both margins, only the left one.*

***DO NOT** ever use indentation, even for effect.*

*And another No: **DO NOT** ever start or end a scene with anything else but descriptions. Dialogue or voice-over should never be written right after a slug-line or directly before the next one.*

Makes sense: How could I hear anything when I have no idea where I am?

But more about that later!

CHAPTER THREE

THE SCENE

YOUR BUILDING BLOCK

"Either a script reads entertainingly and there is a purpose to each scene, or there isn't. And if there isn't a purpose to a scene, it shouldn't be there. If something hasn't changed at the end of the scene from where it began, you're probably not doing your job."

Leslie Dixon
Screenwriter
Outrageous Fortune,
Mrs. Doubtfire,
The Thomas Crown Affair

8/ *Slug/Slug-line/Heading/*

In a screenplay, a scene is a defined element of action, an event or a part of it that takes place inside or outside a given space, in a clearly specified location, at a time precisely delineated or intentionally approximated.

A scene is officially labeled by what professionals call a **slug, slug-line** or **heading**. It's a nutshell description of **how, where** and **when** the action happens in a scene, but not yet **what** will happen, which is what you will introduce in the scene itself.

There are three fundamental elements of information you need to put in your slug: Space (how) location (where) and time (when).

1/ The technical **space** is where an action will take place and how is it conceived and later filmed. This information is important from a production perspective. And it could be one of three:

* An Indoor space, generally surrounded by walls such as a bedroom, a kitchen or an office… Known as **Interior,** and written: INT. in **uppercase, abbreviated and with a period.**

* An outdoor open space, such as a street, a park or a beach… Known as **Exterior,** and written: EXT. in **uppercase, abbreviated and with a period.**

* In some cases it could be a combination of outdoor and indoor spaces. See details later.

2/ The actual physical designation of the **location** where the action takes place could be as general as:

KITCHEN,
PARK,
GARAGE,
HALLWAY,
HOTEL ROOM,
Etc.

Or as specific as:

```
JOHN'S HOUSE,
RICHARD'S BATHROOM,
THE PETERSONS' BACKYARD,
HENNEPIN AVENUE,
Etc.
```

*Whatever your choice, it should be **short**, no more than two or three data, and again, in **uppercase**.*

Lengthy or descriptive information such as the following should be strictly avoided!

===

EXT. THE JACKSON'S BACKYARD ON A BEAUTIFUL FALL DAY,
MINNEAPOLIS, MINNESOTA - DAY

===

*3/ Finally the **time** of the day this particular scene is taking place.*

It could be as general and approximated as:

```
MORNING
DAWN
DAY
AFTERNOON
NIGHT
DUSK
LATER
MOMENTS LATER
LATE AFTERNOON
EARLIER
MOMENTS EARLIER
EARLY MORNING
SUNSET
SUNRISE
CONTINUOUS
```

Or as precise and explicit as:

```
2:34 P.M.
3:15 A.M.
17:45
22:17
NOON
MIDNIGHT
```

The main objective is to give the technicians working on the script an idea about the time of the narrative so that they can appropriately convey it on screen.

But Remember:

There are just a few rules that govern the labeling of a scene; however, you should not mess around with them:

- *All slugs should be **capitalized** but **not bold!***

- *You need to put **one space** between INT. or EXT. and the location!*

- *And: **one space, dash, one space,** between location and time.*

- *Any time you change any of these three fundamental elements, you automatically need to move to a different scene, with a new slug.*

- *Two consecutive scenes should never have the same exact slug. If they do, they should be the same scene. So, you really need to make sure that consecutive scenes, particularly if they happen to take place in the same location, are taking place at clearly different times. Or vice versa…*

Here is how a regular slug/heading should look:

==

INT. ANDERSON'S KITCHEN - DUSK

==

9/ A Particular Note About Space and Location

In very specific cases and for whatever creative need, you could be tempted to combine two spaces, two locations, or both of them in the same slug. Which could help you avoid the repetitious rewriting of the same slugs as you continuously jump from scene to scene, location to location or space to space.

Here are the two most common situations:

1/ You decide to move without actual interruption between inside and outside spaces (or vice-versa) such as with a Steadycam.

2/ You intercut between two characters talking on the phone or connecting with whatever communication device - which means they are in different locations - but for some reason you prefer to show both of them on screen as they speak, maybe looking to emphasize some of their actions or reactions, or using them as counterpoints.

This is how you write the spaces:

EXT./INT.

Or, if the first scene is inside:

INT./EXT.

Both should be **uppercase, abbreviated, with periods** and a **slash** in between.

Same for the actual locations:

You indicate both locations where the actions take place, **uppercase** and a **slash** in between:

BEDROOM/PARK

Or,

PARK/BEDROOM

Depending on which location you actually start with.

Here is an example of an inspired scene between a despondent Richard and an assertive Jane as they fight their lives out:

```
================================================================

EXT./INT. PARK/JANE'S KITCHEN — DAY

Richard and Jane continue their heated conversation over
the phone as Jane prepares her salad and Richard walks
aimlessly through the park, puffing on his hand-rolled
cigarette.

                     RICHARD
          I can't do it right now!


                     JANE
          But you promised, you promised to be
          here for her--


                     RICHARD
                  (Shouting)
          I know I did! But something came up.
          I need to make a living you know--


                     JANE
                  (Hysterical)
          And I need to take care of a child that
          hasn't seen her father in days… Shit!

Jane suddenly cuts herself with the oversized knife.
Lots of blood everywhere!

================================================================
```

Sometimes, to better situate your scene, you might decide to indicate more than one location. In such a case, always start with the largest, followed by the smallest:

```
================================================================

EXT. MINNEAPOLIS - LORING PARK - DAY

================================================================
```

Or,

```
================================================================

INT. ROME, SISTINE CHAPEL, GIFT SHOP — DAY

================================================================
```

*And in any case, **AVOID** redundancies such as:*

```
================================================================

EXT. OUTSIDE PARK — DAY
INT. INSIDE KITCHEN - NIGHT

================================================================
```

If you happen to be in a large location, such as a hotel, a school or a house, understand that each area is actually a different location by itself.

In a hotel, the hallway is different than the bar, the restaurant or any of the rooms. In a house, there is an entrance, a kitchen, a living room, several bedrooms, bathrooms, a foyer, a basement, etc. And a lot could happen in any of these locations. In terms of production, remember that it takes a huge amount of time to move your crew and your equipment from the living room to the kitchen or to the bathroom within the same exact house.

What you usually do is indicate in the first slug the larger location with the specific place we are in, then from there on, simply indicate the particular place where the action happens. Here is the first scene:

```
================================================================

INT. THE HILTON HOTEL, RECEPTION - DAY

================================================================
```

If your following scene happens to be in the same hotel, but in one of the rooms, here is how you it should be written:

```
================================================================

INT. ROOM 716 - DAY

================================================================
```

But some screenwriters like to be more precise and do indicate the larger location anyway. I don't think it would hurt if it makes you feel better…

```
================================================================

INT. HILTON HOTEL, ROOM 716 - DAY

================================================================
```

*If your location happens to be moving, then you should indicate that as well, **in parentheses**, right away in the slug, even if you were to describe the movement later in your directions.*

```
================================================================

INT. CAR (MOVING) - DAY

================================================================
```

Or:

```
================================================================

EXT. CRUISE SHIP (MOVING) - DAY

================================================================
```

10/ A Particular Note About Time

In most cases, the indicated times in a slug are self-explanatory. Some however, in special situations, become problematic or redundant. Others are simply misunderstood by writers who lack any formal production experience and insist on using them. And there are many of those…

Two cases have been causing serious headaches for our students: LATER, or EARLIER, and CONTINUOUS. Their use is definitely subject to specific caveats.

LATER or EARLIER are simply used when one scene happens a short time after, or before, another one. The problem is, what to write when the next scene takes place also a short time after, and the next one as well, and the next one, and the next one…

I have seen too many scripts where, for about a dozen scenes, the times indicated in the slugs were decidedly LATER, and LATER, and LATER. What the heck is actually the LATER of a… preceding LATER, preceded by… another LATER?

Redundant, boring, and amateurish! By that logic, we could easily end up with a script that's filled with… LATERs. After all, when you tell a story chronologically, and the action takes place in a relatively short time such as a day or two, then everything is technically happening, well… LATER.

Besides, by profusely using LATER, or EARLIER, you incur the risk of quickly confusing the technicians reading your script as they end up losing track of DAY and NIGHT scenes. Usually, they will have to go several scenes back to figure out the time of the scene, and you really don't want them to do that for your own sake…

To make any sense, LATER and EARLIER should be preceded by a slug that contains a very defined time.

Such as:

==

INT. ANDERSON'S KITCHEN – DUSK

==

Followed by:

```
================================================================

EXT. ANDERSON'S BACKYARD - LATER

================================================================
```

By the same token, LATER and EARLIER should also be followed by slugs that, again, need to indicate another precisely defined time.

The preceding example should be directly followed by:

```
================================================================

INT. ANDERSON'S BEDROOM - NIGHT

================================================================
```

Unless you wanted to use: MUCH LATER… But how many times could you use that one?

CONTINUOUS is a whole different ballgame.

Beginners, and surprisingly many renowned writers, use it when they try to convey the general feeling of different scenes happening in quick succession, simultaneously, or in some sort of continuity. Others apparently use it when different characters are doing different actions in different places, at more or less the same time. Which is known as parallel actions…

If that's the logic, we again could technically end up with a script made up of CONTINUOUS… When you tell your story chronologically, all events are somehow narrated in a… CONTINUOUS fashion, aren't they? And I have seen a slew of CONINUOUS in many successive scenes, in many "great" scripts as well!

CONTINUOUS *has actually a very specific meaning in screenwriting: a character starts an action at the end of a scene; that same character continues the same exact action in the next scene. Technically we have a continuing action without any loss of time, between two physically contiguous spaces. The idea is that the action is continuing between both spaces as close as possible to real time!*

So, you can't have a CONTINUOUS *between a character starting to open a door in Minneapolis and continuing to open another one in Duluth, two days later. Where is the continuity?*

You can't have a CONTINUOUS *between a character starting to mount a bike in a park and a completely different character mounting a bike on a hill, even if the times were identical… Again, where is the continuity?*

Here is an example of good use of CONTINUOUS:

==

> JENNIFER
> I don't want to talk about it. Just
> leave me alone!

And before Richard could say anything, Jennifer violently OPENS the kitchen door, heads out.

INT. HALLWAY - CONTINUOUS

CHOKING with tears, Jennifer SLAMS the door behind her, CLIMBS the stairs towards the bedroom.

Another door is heard SLAMMING, then nothing.

The kitchen door opens tentatively. Richard walks in, disturbed.

> RICHARD
> Damn it Jennifer!

He slowly moves through the hallway towards the main door.

Another sad and indecisive look upstairs, then he is out!

==

To summarize, CONTINUOUS should not be used if you happen to deal with a different action or a different character, even if they were doing the same action.

Generally, to avoid these pitfalls, it's important to be creative and figure out in advance a continuum of time in your story and how to express it in your scenes, so that the viewer gets an inspired reading experience without repetitious time indications.

11/ Slug Extensions

If needed, you could also include within your slug additional information that stands out of the indicated time or space, such as a specific date or a particular season the viewer needs to be aware of:

```
1947
SUMMER 1952
215 B.C.
31ST CENTURY
FALL
EARLY WINTER
```

In such cases you inform the viewer about that time or season by inserting on screen a title, known as SUPER. But you don't have to, if what you are looking for is to purposefully confuse or stylistically engage the viewer.

Sometimes the additional information could be a specific scene description, an aesthetic choice or a stylistic approach that better qualifies your scene while creating a unique mood:

```
FLASHBACK
DREAM
FLASHFORWARD
FANTASY
NIGHTMARE
VISION
```

*This kind of information, known as **Slug Extension**, should be put in **parentheses**, with **one space** between the parenthesis and the time. Here is how it looks like:*

```
================================================================

INT. ANDERSON'S KITCHEN - DUSK (FLASHBACK - 1947)

================================================================
```

12/ Scene Numbers

*Scenes are generally numbered either on **both sides**, or just on **the left side** of your slug, that is, only **if** you happen to be writing a **director's shooting script**…*

*Since that's usually not your case as a writer, at least not yet, simply **avoid the numbers on any side!***

*I have to admit though: numbering your scenes definitely helps during rewrites, comments and feedback. But I do understand the need to differentiate between yours and the director's draft. The technical, or shooting script will contain numbers, shots, camera movements, and more. Yours **SHOULD NOT** contain any of that. So, stick with the simple slug, without any numbering. Here is how it looks when you write a shooting script:*

```
================================================================

21/ INT. ANDERSON'S KITCHEN - DUSK                         21.

================================================================
```

Or, with numbers just on one side:

```
================================================================

21/ INT. ANDERSON'S KITCHEN - DUSK

================================================================
```

But here is how a slug should look like today, for your regular script, **NOT** *using any numbering at all:*

```
================================================================

INT. ANDERSON'S KITCHEN - DUSK

================================================================
```

13/ Beginnings and Endings:

Whatever the kind of scene you might want to start with, a screenplay **ALWAYS** *starts with a:*

FADE IN:

Yes! **Uppercase, colon** *and set* **flush left.**

Why? Because movies always start from a black screen that slowly fades into the first picture, whatever that picture may be. Thus the FADE IN:

Here is how we start that Oscar script:

```
================================================================

FADE IN:

EXT. DOWNTOWN MINNEAPOLIS - 5:15 P.M.

A scary vista: The MINNEAPOLIS skyline under the most
devastating thunderstorm that has ever been around.

================================================================
```

Comparatively, a screenplay **ALWAYS** *ends with a:*

FADE OUT

*Yes! **Upper case, no colon** and set **flush right**.*

*By the way, **DO NOT** even try to type anything like:*

 END TITLES

Or

THE END

Or

FIN

Or

FINISH

Or whatever other original indication for an ending!

Why? At the end of a movie, the screen goes black, right? So it makes sense to simply use a term that helps convey that exact process. And that is:

FADE OUT

Unless, for some emotional reason or effect you decide to end on a FREEZE FRAME! Then simply write, instead of your traditional FADE OUT:

FREEZE FRAME

Here is how your Oscar movie ends…

===

Richard dashes along the runway as the old plane takes off, RATTLING right over his head.

He runs with all his might…

And runs…

Suddenly, the plane veers back for a short moment.

Richard is puzzled.

But before he realizes, two gunshots EXPLODE from the cockpit, with a deadly precision.

Richard runs some more, in slow motion, like a disconnected puppet, COLLAPSES!

For the longest time of his life…

The plane veers again, and disappears in the skies.

                                        FADE OUT

===

14/ What if I Started Differently?

Sometimes, because of whatever mood you wish to create, you might decide to start your script on a black, white or otherwise colored screen with a narration or any quirky sound effects you choose.

In such a case, you should not begin with the traditional FADE IN: since you technically have only one part of your opening scene, the sound. So, don't use a complete slug. Start rather with one the following:

BLACK SCREEN
BLACKNESS
GREEN SCREEN
BLUE SCREEN

Or whatever screen color you wish to present to the viewer, for whatever creative reason.

And again, remember: **Upper case, colon** and **flush left.** Then describe what the viewer will hear in the sound track in your regular directions.

As soon as you are ready to show your first picture, just go back to the traditional FADE IN: and start your regular slug after a double space.

Here is how it goes:

==

BLACK SCREEN:

It's RAINING cats and dogs!

Suddenly the RATTLING of thunder EXPLODES. Long and ominous…

The rain doubles in intensity as a SIREN speeds somewhere in the streets.

FADE IN:

EXT. DOWNTOWN MINNEAPOLIS — 5:15 P.M.

A scary vista: the Minneapolis skyline under the most devastating thunderstorm that has ever been around…

SUPER: MINNEAPOLIS — SUMMER 1999

                    NARRATOR (V.O.)
          Who could have imagined that a stupid
          Midwestern storm could radically change
          the course of one's life…

Another flash of lightning lacerates the skies, followed by deafening THUNDER.

                                        FADE TO WHITE

==

15/ My take, so far!

I agree: what you have been reading so far looks pretty much like a long litany of rules to abide by and not at all what you bargained for in the first place.

I already see the glossy eyes of many disappointed students: you intended to write the next amazing script and here you end up with rules and regulations at every step of the way…

I understand the frustration! To put things into perspective, here is how two professionals see this conundrum.

Paul Marcus,** the Producer of **Prime Suspect 2** strictly stresses one aspect: **"If a script is not correctly formatted, even with the best will in the world, I'm reading it negatively from the start because I'm thinking: this person is unprofessional, they haven't even bothered to take the time to find how it should be laid out. It doesn't have to be glossy, just easily readable."

Bob Bookman,** an agent at CAA, on the other hand gives a lot of hope for the unruly: **"I think rules are adhered to by hacks. The best writers learn the literal rules of their craft, then break those rules and become great writers."

My take is simple, as I happen to not always follow the rules myself: go ahead, break the rules! But I found through my career that the best way to break the rules is to learn them first, then learn how to break them!

Just a thought…

CHAPTER FOUR

LET'S WALK THE WALK

"It's a mistake to get hung up on numbers. Writing a script is not a joining the dots operation or getting the numbers right. Allow the story to dictate its own requirements. The "numbers" you get on many courses or in various books should be used to develop your storytelling instincts, to validate your guesses and intuitions, and then forget them. Learn them, then throw them away."

David Webb Peoples
Screenwriter
Unforgiven
Blade Runner
Twelve Monkeys

16/ *Visualization*

Painters need canvasses to paint, sculptors use bronze or stone to chisel, poets play with words to create rhymes, and musicians revel in notes to bring us memorable tunes.

Is it then surprising that screenwriters need a screen on which they can project the images they create? That screen is nothing else but the page of the script! Each word, each sentence you put on that page conveys an image I can see or a sound I can hear as I read the script.

*Thus the need to be "**visual**", to create directions that translate automatically into pictures, to avoid thoughts that no one obviously can see! Thus the basic rule you must follow when writing your directions: **If I cannot see it, if I cannot hear it, it cannot be on the page!***

*Describing a scene actually means allowing me to **see** the location where your characters happen to be doing or saying something. So: **If you don't write anything, I cannot see anything.** If you just write some dialogue directly after your slug, without any kind of direction, it simply means there is a blank screen!*

*That's why, as a rule, you should **NEVER** write in your directions such sentences as:*

```
================================================================

We see Richard entering the hotel room.

Then you hear a ROARING sound in the backyard.

================================================================
```

That would be pretty redundant! By simply writing:

```
================================================================

Richard enters the hotel room.

Suddenly a ROARING erupts in the backyard.

================================================================
```

I actually see Richard enter the room and I hear the roaring sound the moment it is written on the page.

*So, there should not be any "**we**" or "**you**" in a script… And the same goes for any verb after We or You, such as we see or we move or we hear. "We" or "you" are not part of the screen…*

17/ Presentification

*To help with visualization, screenwriting calls for "presentification" or the art of creating directions exclusively in the **present and active tense.** As opposed to literature, poetry, journalism, or any other form of writing, a writer should never use any other tense but the present!*

Makes sense: As a reader, I am watching actions that are happening right now in front of me, on my personal screen, created by the screenwriter. So how could there be any past, future or subjunctive?

Here is how it should look:

==

INT. HOTEL ROOM — NIGHT

Cold, cheap…

Richard THROWS his suitcase on the tiny bed, rushes to the air conditioner.

It comes to life as he PUSHES the ON button, for maybe two seconds, SPUTTERS, COUGHS and wilts down in a whirl of SCREECHING sounds.

Richard SIGHS: This is not going to be a good night…

==

*And here is what you should **NEVER** write:*

```
================================================================

INT. HOTEL ROOM — NIGHT

Cold, cheap…

Richard has THROWN his suitcase on the tiny bed and rushed
to the air conditioner.

It came to life as Richard PUSHED the ON button, for maybe
two seconds. The engine SPUTTERED, COUGHED and wilted down
in a whirl of SCREECHING sounds.

Richard SIGHED: This was not going to be a good night…

================================================================
```

See how the consistent use of the past tense takes the reader away from the action; we are not visually witnessing the action on screen, we are merely being informed about it. We seem to be part of something that has already happened in a past time and we are wondering what is actually happening on screen while we are told about Richard and his predicament. This example is very literary and not at all visual, cinematic!

18/ Economy

Economy is another fundamental rule to help us create visually powerful directions. It relates to the amount of words we use to describe characters, actions, sounds or locations. Directions have to be as succinct as possible, with a lot of empty space in between, very short lines and as many paragraphs as you can afford for a better reading experience.

Paddy Chayevsky, *the famed writer of such amazing scripts as **Being There** and **Network,** was absolutely ruthless when it came to his own writing: **"First cut out all the wisdom, then cut out all the adjectives. I've cut some of my favorite stuff. I have no real compassion when it comes to cutting: No pity, no sympathy. Some of my dearest and***

most beloved bits of writing have gone out with a very quick slash, slash, slash."

If it makes you happier, look at it this way: They really don't have time to read that many scripts in Tinsel Town as indicated in the introduction of this text!

But I wish this were the only reason.

So, why this emphasis on economy in screenwriting, as opposed to, say literature?

*Because directions are not meant to be a grocery shop list you present to the viewer! You don't have to describe every single item in your space. All you have to do is give the reader a sense of how that location feels, create what we call **the mood** or **the feel** of the place.*

And sometimes this will take just one sentence! Good screenwriters are known for their tremendous ability to encapsulate complicated descriptions in very succinct sentences that surprisingly say a lot, and they say it very visually.

Another reason why we do not need the expanse of details is simple: someone else in the crew (the director, the production designer, the art director, the director of Photography, etc.) will ultimately fill the space you created with all that it needs, based on your short and pertinent descriptions.

*That's what's known as **collaborative work**! Many a talented artists will create, based on your descriptions, their own vision of what will ultimately shape visually and aurally the final movie on screen. Cinema is definitely the epitome of collaboration between artists, and screenwriting happens to be its first step.*

Sure, grammar and spelling are essential, but economy is definitely the key word. Even sentence fragments are acceptable in screenwriting, often preferred, despite good grammar.

*In short, **less is more**, as they say.*

Here is how one of my students described the disgusting, smelly and tiny bedroom of his protagonist.

```
================================================================
```

INT. RICHARD'S BEDROOM — LATE NIGHT

A large bed that has seen it all sits in the corner of the
tiny bedroom, undone. A mound of mismatched sheets, pillows
and a bedspread, smelly, repugnant and cigarette-burned,
towers in the center.

To the right, on an improvised night table made of a
turned-up crate, an ashtray bursts with burned cigarette
butts and joints. Some are distinctively smeared with marks
of all sorts of lipstick: green, red burgundy and… black!

A small wobbly table in the other corner of the room is
filled with the most unpredictable items: Two CD's by KISS,
a small bong, a keychain, a dildo, two yellow-striped
condoms, a knife, an antique revolver from the 1800's, a
pizza box with the rest of a wedge surrounded by two
devouring rats, a rosary and a mini-bible.

To the right, a sink, filled with dirty dishes and scraps
of all sorts of smelly food, sits in the middle of the
other wall. It is surrounded by a swarm of BUZZING flies,
more rats and an army of cockroaches fighting over an
improbable meal.

A carpet, discolored and badly stained, yellowed in places,
shagged in others, partly covers what must have been a
wooden floor many, many years ago.

No windows anywhere in this tiny, barely nine by nine
bedroom. The only exit is a door, badly broken following
some violent outburst. And along one of its sides, a bunch
of corroded chains and locks, one built over the other,
convey a laughable and futile effort for protection.

Suddenly, the sound of a LOCK being tortured is heard and
the door comes to life as Richard PUSHES it and enters.

He quickly SLAMS the door and hastily LOCKS all the chains
in a cacophony of metallic SHRIEKS.

```
================================================================
```

OK! You get the point…

Do I really need to know all of these details? Are they truly that important to my story? Would the future viewer of the movie miss anything if this scene were written more concisely?

The answer to all of these questions is probably no. True, some of the details might be needed to understand how the events will progress in the story. Those you ought to reveal. But it is essential to not overwhelm your reader with details that you will never use later.

Here is how that same student who went on to become an excellent screenwriter, ended up economically rewriting the scene in a more exciting script, while trying to point the attention of the viewer to important details in the story:

==

INT. RICHARD'S BEDROOM — LATE NIGHT

A tiny, windowless, filthy prison-like enclosure.

On a disgusting garbage-laden sink, rats and cockroaches fight over scraps of dried pizza.

A messy bed and a rickety night table face a broken door laden with corroded chains and locks.

Suddenly, the sound of a LOCK, hurried and insistent!

The door comes to life as Richard PUSHES his way in.

He quickly SLAMS it, hastily LOCKS all the chains in a cacophony of metallic SHRIEKS.

==

The need to be economical in your directions could go even further when you deal with generic locations that all of us have a pretty good idea of, thanks to real life, movies, television or simply empirical knowledge.

When you write:

```
EXT. PARK
INT. CLASSROOM
INT. HOTEL ROOM
INT. AIRPORT TERMINAL
EXT. CRUISE SHIP DECK
```

You have already created a picture in the reader's mind. All you need following your slug is a succinct description to convey the mood of that particular hotel room, park or airport terminal. Then move on with your action and tell your story.

Unless there is something unique about your location: this is not the usual classroom you might have in mind, this terminal has a particular feel to it, this deck is stylish but it has a tacky aspect, etc.

Otherwise, don't spend your time describing what everyone knows about a classroom or a terminal, just tell us what is unique about these particular ones.

==

INT. CLASSROOM — DAY

Tiny, dark and deserted… This is not where you want your kid to spend eight hours a day.

EXT. CRUISE SHIP DECK — DAY

Posh and stylish… An army of WAITERS seems to compete for one's tiniest wishes. Right upfront, a chic heart-shaped pool, pink, with tacky mauve stripes.

Badly burned bodies scattered amid gallons of martinis and margaritas, and the stench of humongous Cuban cigars.

INT. AIRPORT TERMINAL - DAY

Frantic, crowded and definitely without air conditioning… Tempers seem ready to flare, as the line in front of the gate keeps getting longer.

The SECURITY OFFICER, a jaded older man with a face that
has seen it all, scrutinizes every single item in every
single suitcase.

===

To summarize, you should write simple and succinct
sentences. Here is what helps:

AVOID conjunctions such as **and** or **then**, simple commas
will suffice.

AVOID stacking related actions on top of each
other logically.

TRY TO AVOID being redundant. Once you have made
your point, move on!

Here is an example of what you should **NOT** write:

===

INT. HOTEL ROOM — NIGHT

Richard enters. He THROWS his suitcase on the tiny bed and
approaches the air conditioner.

He PUSHES the ON button and it comes to LIFE, but no cold
air seems to be coming through. Richard PUSHES more buttons
and the air conditioner starts to SPUTTER and COUGH and
then, it wilts down in a whirl of SCREECHING sounds.

Richard SIGHS. His face turns sour as he realizes the
terrible night ahead of him.

===

Here is a better version, avoiding redundancies, some
of the conjunctions, applying the economy with short and
pertinent sentences:

```
================================================================

INT. HOTEL ROOM — NIGHT

Cold, cheap...

Richard THROWS his suitcase on the tiny bed, rushes to the
air conditioner.

It comes to life as he PUSHES the ON button, for maybe two
seconds. Then SPUTTERS, COUGHS and wilts down in a whirl of
SCREECHING sounds.

Richard SIGHS: This is not going to be a good night...

================================================================
```

Unfortunately, in trying to shorten their sentences, dilettantes usually get in conflict with basic grammar. Sometimes they go so far as trimming all articles and pronouns, thinking this would make their prose hip and cool. What they end up creating is a mishmash of weird and broken English, very comparable to a bad police report or a stupidly crafted telegram.

Too much trimming is just... too much.

*Here is what you should **NEVER** write:*

```
================================================================

INT. HOTEL ROOM — NIGHT

Cold, cheap...

Richard THROWS suitcase on bed. Rushes to air conditioner.
PUSHES ON button.

Air Conditioner comes to life. No cold air.

PUSHES more buttons. Air conditioner SPUTTERS, COUGHS,
wilts down. SCREECHING sounds.
```

Richard SIGHS. Face sour. Terrible night ahead!

==

19/ Of Verbs and Actions

Another issue that you need to carefully consider when it comes to crafting your directions is the choice of words: nouns, verbs, adverbs, adjectives, articles or pronouns, etc. Given what we were just discussing, they all need to be short, expressive, and mostly visual! When read, they need to immediately convey a strong picture. As opposed to literature where your words can convey a mood or a thought, we already know that in screenwriting we can write only what's visual.

So we really need to spend some time to find the exact words that actually emphasize the visual while helping create the mood of the general script. Here is how **Larry Fergusson**, the famed writer of **The Hunt For Red October**, **Alien** and **Beverly Hills Cop II** sees this eternal quest for strong visual actions: **"Always ask yourself if you can find a stronger, more specific verb. People don't just enter a room, they storm in, they bang in, they creep in, and they crawl in! Emphasize the visual."**

20/ Directions Between Pages

Long time ago, when a scene continued from one page to the next, you needed to write in the lower right-hand corner of the first page, two spaces after the very last line:

(CONTINUED)

In **parentheses** and **uppercase**!

On the following page, in the upper left-hand corner, you had to start with:

CONTINUED:

*In **Uppercase, without parentheses** but with a **colon!***

After double-spacing, you continue with your direction or dialogue. Here is how it looked then:

```
==================================================================

                          JENNIFER
              I don't want to talk about it. Just
              leave me alone!

Overwhelmed with tears, she quickly walks out of the
kitchen, SLAMMING the door behind her.

Richard STOPS his packing, unable to move for a long
moment. His anger suddenly seems to mount as he grabs a

                                        (CONTINUED)

-------------------------Next Page-------------------------

                                              16.

CONTINUED:

large China vase from the table, SMASHES it through the
window.

==================================================================
```

Here is how it looks now and notice the amount of space you actually gained:

```
==================================================================

                          JENNIFER
              I don't want to talk about it. Just
              leave me alone!
```

Overwhelmed with tears, she quickly walks out of the
kitchen, SLAMMING the door behind her.

Richard STOPS his packing, unable to move for a long
moment. His anger suddenly seems to mount as he grabs a

-----------------------Next Page------------------------

16.

large China vase from the table, SMASHES it through the
window.

==

As a rule, **NEVER** end a page with a slug dangling alone
without an actual direction; at least one line of dialogue
or direction should be written.

Here is the atrocious case to **AVOID**:

==

EXT. /INT. PARK/JANE'S KITCHEN — DAY

-----------------------Next Page------------------------

Richard and Jane continue their heated conversation over
the phone as Jane prepares her salad and Richard walks
aimlessly through the park, puffing on his hand-rolled
cigarette.

==

If you inadvertently find yourself without room for
even one line of description, the best you can do is to
move your slug to the next page altogether.

21/ Transitions

Simply defined, transition pertains to the way you move visually and aurally from one scene to another. For some strange reason, beginners always feel the urge to find sophisticated ways to transit from scene to scene.

The reality is, if you are not careful about using transitions, you will end up meddling not only with the director's turf, but actually with the editor's as well, and they frankly both hate that.

*Definitely **all** of the following transitions are a poor and laughable attempt on the part of a would-be writer to impress the reader with doubtful technical bravura. Most of them most of the time frankly just make no sense, except for the dilettante and the uneducated:*

CUT TO:
Proudly used by some screenwriters as either an uncommon or a regular transition at the end of a scene.

Look at it this way: What would happen if you don't write CUT TO:? Would the picture stop there waiting for your input? Guess what, nothing would happen! Whether you like it or not, there will still be a cut right there, just as there were many other cuts you were not aware of. That's how film works. That's what film as an art is all about: editing consecutive shots together!

*And don't even try to give me this **"abrupt and emotional cut between two scenes"** baloney, as some want to define CUT TO: What could be more abrupt than a cut between two shots?*

Again, people who have never touched a foot of film, never spliced two shots in their lives, or experienced the exhilaration of creating a new reality by connecting shots together, will obviously have difficulties understanding what a CUT or a CUT TO: means…

To summarize: Mr., Mrs. or Ms. Screenwriter, guys and gals, you need to shoot, produce, cut and edit! How could you write for the screen, if you have never experienced that screen?

SMASH CUT:

What the heck is that? How is it any different than a regular cut? Do you have a clue how "smashing" is any given cut between two shots?

SLAM CUT:

*What was that again? You are **slamming** a shot over another… How more powerful than a regular is that?*

SHOCK CUT:

Oh Brother! It's just… shocking!

MATCH CUT:

*Excuse me? I know **Action Match Cut**, which is a cut between two different angles of the same action using the character's movement as a transition. Is it supposed to be the same as Match Cut? If that's the case, then you are way into deciding not only the shots, but also how to edit them at the end. One person is supposed to be doing that, and that's not you Mr. Screenwriter!*

MATCH DISSOLVE:

Re-excuse me? Never heard of that one!

LAP DISSOLVE:

Go figure what that one is…

WIPE TO:

Yeah sure, that's exactly how the director will film it, just to please you!

IRIS IN:

Really! Go ahead, dream on and see how the director will react!

IRIS OUT:

Sure, continue dreaming on!

The amazing fact with most of these weird names is if you asked a director, a director of photography, an editor or any knowledgeable technician, they would probably have no clue what the heck you are talking about.

And that's perfectly understandable: open any glossary and I dare you to find any of these mysterious terms. Which leads us to a simple fact: terms like Smash Cut, Slam Cut or *Match Dissolve* could have been created only by clueless screenwriters trying to impress the gallery.

Simply stated: **NOTHING** is usually needed to transit between scenes! And that nothing is actually a simple, clear, neat cut between the last shot of a scene and the first shot of the following one. Which translates in the page as… **NOTHING** between two scenes!

Now if you wanted to be more… let's say expressive… or creative… a very few technical transitions should be used and only if they truly help convey a better mood or effect for your storytelling.

Here are the ones you could use without attracting the ire of anybody:


```
FADE OUT
FADE IN:
DISSOLVE
FADE TO BLACK (or WHITE)
```


Not much, as you see, since the rest is really not your business: off limits as it were.

But if you do decide to use any of the indicated transitions, set them **flush right,** at the **end of a scene** and **double-spaced.**

Here is Jennifer walking out on Richard:


```
================================================================

                          JENNIFER
            I don't want to talk about it. Just
            leave me alone!

Overwhelmed with tears, Jennifer quickly walks out of the
kitchen, SLAMMING the door behind her.

                                              DISSOLVE:
```

EXT. HENNEPIN AVENUE — AFTERNOON

Jennifer, still in tears, walks aimlessly through the
afternoon crowd. Zombies leaving their boring jobs,
rushing back into their monotonous lives… She bumps into
few of them without even realizing their presence.

==

By the way, remember that if you:

                                                             FADE OUT

At the end of a given scene, you need to:

FADE IN:

Flush left, before you start the next one.

*Make sense, doesn't it? I am still under the effect of
the black screen after a FADE OUT, until you actually tell
me that we are going into a new scene, and open the screen
with a FADE IN:*

*Here is a slightly different emotional feeling to the
earlier scene:*

==

                           JENNIFER
                I don't want to talk about it. Just
                leave me alone!

Overwhelmed with tears, Jennifer quickly walks out of the
kitchen SLAMMING the door behind her.

                                                    FADE OUT

FADE IN:

```
EXT. - HENNEPIN AVENUE - AFTERNOON

Jennifer, still in tears, walks aimlessly through the
afternoon crowd. Zombies leaving their boring jobs, rushing
back into their monotonous lives… She bumps into few of
them without even realizing their presence.

==============================================================
```

22/ *What About the Technical Stuff*

Yeah… what about that technical stuff?

Simple: Definitely, with no pity or sympathy, all the technical terms, such as:

```
PAN
DOLLY
TRACK
ZOOM IN
ZOOM OUT
REVERSE ANGLE
ANGLE ON
ESTABLISHING SHOT
LONG SHOT
MEDIUM SHOT
CLOSE UP
CLOSE ON
ON…
CUT TO
SMASH CUT
SLAM CUT
SHOCK CUT
MATCH CUT
JUMP CUT
MOS
INSERT
WIPE
IRIS
P.O.V.
BACK TO:
```

*Should be **STRICTLY AVOIDED!***

Again, and I hate to keep repeating this: **it's not your job, it's the director's!** *He/she will later, once you are done with your successive drafts, insert the technical directions in the shooting script.*

John Milius, *acclaimed writer* **of Apocalypse Now, 1941** *and* **Clear and Present Danger** *sees it in very simple terms:* **"I never write shot descriptions, never say "We pull in" or "We see". How presumptuous to say that sort of thing. The only useful thing about the screenplay form is to tell you whether it's day or night, inside or outside. Everything else should be like a novel — clean and sharp and interesting to read."**

I am not necessarily crazy about the novel-like comparison… But you get the point. Technical descriptions are really not your turf!

This said, some specific technical terms have entered the screenwriting pantheon and became part of the jargon a writer could use with impunity:

```
FADE IN:
FADE OUT
DISSOLVE: or DISSOLVE TO:
FLASHBACK
FLASHFORWARD
DREAM
NIGHTMARE
FANTASY
TITLE CARD or TITLE
BLACK SCREEN or BLACKNESS
SUPER or SUPERIMPOSE
SPLIT SCREEN
MONTAGE
SERIES OF SHOTS
INSERT
```

The reason is simple: As moviegoers have become savvier and more technically aware, these particular directions have gradually become simple indications informing the reader about the scene progression or transition.

They also help create the mood.

However, in the first list, a definite directorial decision is made and the future director might or might not agree with it. They usually will not.

Here is that Oscar worthy example with the correct use of allowable technical terms:

```
================================================================

FADE IN:

EXT. DOWNTOWN MINNEAPOLIS - 5:15 P.M. (FLASHBACK)

A scary vista of the MINNEAPOLIS skyline under the most
devastating thunderstorm of all time…

SUPER: MINNEAPOLIS - SUMMER 1999

                        NARRATOR (V.O.)
            Who could have imagined that a stupid
            Midwestern storm could change so
            radically the course of one's life...

Another lightning bolt lacerates the skies, followed by
deafening THUNDER. The rain DOUBLES in intensity.

                                          FADE TO WHITE
================================================================
```

23/ Montage

*Simply stated, **Montage** is the French word for editing! That means, editing shots together so that a filmmaker can narrate a story in a movie.*

As the screenwriting profession progressed, the concept of Montage slowly evolved into a storytelling device where a compilation of short visuals from different locations and/or times is used to convey a specific idea or an association of ideas, or create a particular emotional effect. It could be a progressive development in the story or the events, the passage of time, the gradual change of a situation or relationship, or simply the transformation of a character following some psychological upheaval.

A montage is labeled as one unified scene with the few permutations of the following slug-line:

INT./EXT. MONTAGE — DAY/NIGHT

If your first action is INT. *and* DAY

INT./EXT. MONTAGE — NIGHT/DAY

If your first action is INT. *and* NIGHT

EXT./INT. MONTAGE — DAY/NIGHT

If your first action is EXT. *and* DAY

EXT./INT. MONTAGE — NIGHT/DAY

If your first action is EXT. *and* NIGHT

Unless all the actions take place inside or outside, and all the actions happen at night or during the day. The slug then might look like this:

INT. MONTAGE - DAY

Or

EXT. MONTAGE — NIGHT

Sometimes screenwriters like to be more specific about the montage itself and in which geographic area it takes place. So, do not be surprised to find a slug like the following:

EXT. MONTAGE AROUND ROME — DAY

All the actions in a montage are introduced one by one with bullets (*), numbers (1/, 2/, 3/, etc.), letters (A/, B/, C/, etc.) or simple dashes (- or --), clearly described into very short and double-spaced paragraphs

In a montage, the idea, the mood or the progressive change we want to convey, are created by using different characters doing different actions in different times and in different spaces. That variety is what makes it a… montage of actions that add up to an idea, a mood or a progressive change in behavior or relationship.

Actually, that's the basic principle of editing, which is at the core of the entire cinematic storytelling process.

Here is an example of a montage:

===

EXT./INT. MONTAGE - DAY

1/ A crowd gathered in front of a BEST BUY watches with horror the many TV screens blasting warnings over the map of the region. Red flashing words TORNADO WATCH blink intermittently.

2/ The streets leading to the only out of town highway are packed with cars and trucks, filled with boxes and other worldly possessions. A POLICEMAN tries to direct backed up traffic. Tensions flair.

3/ A FATHER and a SON hastily NAIL large wooden boards over the windows of their poorly maintained older house.

4/ In a half-emptied grocery store, CUSTOMERS pack their carts high with water, bread, meats and other basic necessities, pushing each other in a fight for life…

===

I am sure you get through this montage the urgent and panicked mood on the island, but also what people are doing to face the impending tornado.

Here is another example where the relationship between Jennifer and Richard progresses through a montage:

```
================================================================

EXT. MONTAGE/MINNEAPOLIS - DAY

A/ Richard and Jennifer sip coffee in a CARIBOU Coffee
Shop's outside patio, entranced in tentative conversation.

B/ Richard and Jennifer walk hand in hand over the STONE
ARCH BRIDGE, LAUGHING at Richard's unheard joke, seemingly
relaxed.

C/ Richard and Jennifer enter the WALKER ARTS CENTER, with
Richard's hand around Jennifer's shoulders.

D/ On the porch of her apartment, Richard tentatively moves
his lips to kiss Jennifer. She first sheepishly responds,
but quickly succumbs into a passionate kiss.


================================================================
```

Pretty straightforward! Here are however a few caveats when you use a montage:

- *One of the fundamental rules when using a montage is to **AVOID** as much as possible the use of music or dialogue. For good reasons: the short actions you describe will be cut very soon by other actions in other places or times.*

- *As for the music, any music you indicate will be cut abruptly by the next action as well. You **DO NOT** want to include a bunch of quick bits of music intercut in a very cacophonic way. Remember also that usually a montage will probably end up being under some non-diegetic music created when the movie is scored, which is not your job, obviously.*

- *In terms of dialogue, you simply will not have enough time for an exchange of lines during the short described actions, unless it is a quick and simple word uttered by the characters, immediately understandable and repeated enough to help convey the idea you are trying to convey. Otherwise, simply **AVOID IT!***

- *Finally, you might find in some illustrious scripts*

the words END OF MONTAGE at the actual end of a montage. **DO NOT** *ever use END OF MONTAGE! This, again, was fomented by screenwriters without any production experience! When you finish the last action of your montage, simply go to your next scene, put a slug-line and move on.* **A montage is a scene like any other scene, DO NOT treat it differently!**

24/ Series of Shots

Montage is sometimes wrongly slugged as Series of Shots. A **Series of Shots** *generally shows the same character doing different actions in different times but within the same space. The best example would be your hero at home, going through different actions, as she/he gets ready to leave to work, or as he/she readies the house for the person they have invited.*

A series of shots is slugged just like a montage:

INT./EXT. SERIES OF SHOTS - DAY/NIGHT

If your first action is INT. and DAY

INT./EXT. SERIES OF SHOTS - NIGHT/DAY

If your first action is INT. and NIGHT

EXT./INT. SERIES OF SHOTS - DAY/NIGHT

If your first action is EXT. and DAY

EXT./INT. SERIES OF SHOTS - NIGHT/DAY

If your first action is EXT. and NIGHT

But if all the actions take place inside or outside, night or day. The slug then might look like this:

INT. SERIES OF SHOTS - DAY

Or

EXT. SERIES OF SHOTS - NIGHT

All the montage rules introduced above precisely apply to the series of shots. Here is an example with Richard getting ready for his big date with Jennifer:

==

INT/EXT. SERIES OF SHOTS — DAY/NIGHT

A/ Richard THROWS finely cut pieces of meat into a pot. It SIZZLES furiously. The steam fills the cooking area.

B/ In the dining corner, Richard carefully places cheap china on a tiny dining table. He thinks twice about how to put the silverware, but ends up just piling it on one side of the plate.

C/ In front of a dusted mirror, he carefully puts on a brand new shirt. It's all wrinkled and he does not seem to like it. He pulls on the sides, tucks it under his pants and it seems to do the trick.

D/ Richard lights two long stem candles in front of the plates, puts a bouquet of red roses in a cheap glass vase.

E/ As he tries the food in the kitchen corner, the bell RINGS. He jumps back, the spaghetti sauce flies all around, SPLATTERS on his new shirt!

He SIGHS, the bell RINGS again.

==

CHAPTER FIVE

<u>LET'S TALK THE TALK</u>

"Italian Director Lina Wertmuller (Swept Away, Seven Beauties) takes a completed screenplay and rewrites every scene without any dialogue. She replaces her dialogue with visual storytelling, using images instead of words. Then she does a final draft of the script, a conglomerate of the most successful images she invented for the story (that replaced dialogue now no longer necessary) and whatever dialogue must remain for the story line. In this way she insures that her films will be first and foremost visual experiences."

Reported by
Charles Deemer

25/ Dialogue And Conversation

Dialogue, also known as **lines**, are the words spoken by any given character, whether seen or not, either addressing someone we see or not, talking over some communication device or simply **thinking out loud**...

Dialogue is not the traditional conversation we use in our daily lives with other human beings! As opposed to how we speak in real life, dialogue is more purposeful and more structured, for a good reason: it happens to be one of the elements that help us express the drama; it helps the characters to communicate, it helps to motivate and justify their actions, it helps to reveal and expose elements of their lives, it helps to create conflict, infuse emotions, and it definitely helps with motivation, intent, purpose, plot, backstory, time, place, etc.

But there is more to the lines in a script: we could spend two hours chatting about mostly nothing in real life; just visit any bar and you will witness that. But can we afford that in a movie? Obviously not, or we will end up with twenty-hour movies... Now how exciting is that?

Movie dialogue is actually very stylized; the words we put in the mouth of our characters have to be precise, expressive, filled with subtext and purpose, designed to convey defined emotions and most importantly, should be as succinct as possible, given the fact that sometimes we have to tell life stories in less than two hours of screen time. Screenwriters spend countless hours chiseling very short lines to reach the exact emotional effect they are seeking.

However: polishing your dialogue makes sense only if you have a good story to tell. Dialogue should never take precedence over the basic storytelling process. Studio executives, who read scripts every single day, are very suspicious of crafty dialogue that stands on its own without the structured story that should sustain it.

Leslie Dixon, writer of such hits as **Outrageous Fortune, Mrs. Doubtfire** and **The Thomas Crown Affair**, puts it in these sobering terms: **"All the witty dialogue of the world in a script in which nothing is happening is still going to make them [the executives] put it away before they get to the end. All the care you lavish on these little witty exchanges is really the least important thing in a studio's mind."**

Mark Valenti, a Hollywood Story Analyst, basically agrees: "Thumb through your scripts, and if you see a lot of black ink in massive areas, cut it. Learn to kill your babies. Even if you're getting rid of the funniest monologue in the universe, if it's not essential to carry the story forward, cut it."

To summarize, the basic principle remains the same: dialogue is not conversation!

This said, here are a few helpful technical hints to put your lines properly on the page:

26/ Characters' Names/Characters' Slugs

The name of a character that speaks, also known as a character slug, is always uppercase and written 2.5 inches from the left margin. No period or colon is ever required after the character's slug!

Dialogue is traditionally written one space after the name, squeezed between 1 and 5 inches from your left margin. It looks like this:

```
================================================================

                    RICHARD
          Pretty fancy. Looks like Better Homes
          and Garden. Where's Stacy?

                    ELEANOR
                   (Impatient)
          I don't know… Upstairs.

================================================================
```

Just like for real people, you need to give your characters some names. Although you are free to choose any quirky name your character will feel comfortable or uncomfortable with, a few rules still apply:

- *Names should generally be as short as possible: JOHN, MARY or EVA. But they could also be vague when we deal with supporting or one-string characters that appear rarely or only once in the whole script: BARMAN, DRIVER, CABBIE, SECRETARY or COP.*

- *If your character's name is MARY PETERSON or ALAN JOHNSON, you better choose MARY or PETERSON, ALAN or JOHNSON in the character slug. But don't ever jump between both: You should refer to a character always by the same exact name throughout the entire script.*

- *When dealing with a multitude of characters in a script, it is recommended that you choose names that are not comparable in spelling or pronunciation: JOHN and JON are confusing to the reader and ultimately the viewer. So are BETH and BETTY, ANDERSON and ANDERSEN, CATHY and KATHY, LOUIS and LOUIE, ALEX and ALEX, DEAN and DEANE, CHRIS and KRIS, BOBBI and BOBBY or JOE and JO…*

- *In character slugs, it's preferable **NOT** to include professional titles like DR. JOHNSON, CAPT. BLAKE or PROF. OLSON… Slug them rather as JOHNSON, BLAKE or OLSON when they speak.*

- *Occasionally, for dramatic purposes or simply because it takes time to know your character, you might want to introduce someone with one name and later discover or uncover their real name. In such cases avoid giving away prematurely the mystery or the surprise.*

  So, don't write something like this:

==

The Drunkard, in reality JIMMY RESTINHELL disguised, sits beside Richard as he turns to address the Barman.

==

Or…

```
================================================================
```

Mary Knowitall, posing as EVA THE STRIPPER, pushes the door of the posh nightclub open.

```
================================================================
```


Remember that your readers are supposed to be unaware, just like your viewers. They are to uncover the truth at the very exact time you decide it is appropriate, not before or after. Otherwise, you lose your effect as well as the emotion you meant to create.

It is thus recommended that you use the name you introduce a particular character with, say BARMAN or SECRETARY, as long as dramatically needed. Later, when it is discovered that they are actually DETECTIVE CONRAD or EVA THE STRIPPER, you then describe the discovery clearly in your directions, and use, if there is a dialogue, a transitional character slug like:

SECRETARY/EVA THE STRIPPER

Before you start slugging the new name.

Here is how it looks without dialogue:

```
================================================================
```

The Drunkard looks at Richard for a long moment. Richards avoids his stare. The drunkard suddenly SNAPS his own beard with a quick motion.

SWOOSH!

He SLAMS the elaborate contraption on the table, stares at Richard: This is actually JIMMY RESTINHELL, disguised.

```
================================================================
```

Here is another case with dialogue:

```
================================================================

EVA THE STRIPPER, all curves and boobs and satin, PUSHES
open the door of the posh nightclub.

As she turns toward the light, her face glistens with fear:
this is really Joel's secretary!

She approaches a bored BOUNCER.

                    EVA THE STRIPPER/SECRETARY
          Hi, I am here to see Joel…

                    BOUNCER
          Name?

                    SECRETARY
          EVA… Eva Longoria…

                    BOUNCER
          Sure… And I am Brad Pitt!

================================================================
```

27/ Economy Again, With a Dilemma!

As opposed to directions, you should never separate your dialogue in paragraphs, even if long. And dialogue should never be long; it is generally hard to read long lines and it is even harder today to find actors who could deliver long speeches properly! Most of the current stars are barely able to remember two consecutive lines…

So, what to do with longer speeches, if they happen to be absolutely necessary?

The best is to break them up with appropriate bits of actions, particularly if these actions are dramatically significant, thematically allegoric or deeply symbolic. And even if you decided to emulate the strict reality of people boringly spending their lives away with insipid dialogue, you should remember that they like to do so while they are going through different actions, as inane as they might be.

*This said, the operating rule when creating dialogue is again **economy**, even more so than with directions.*

Makes sense: scripts are first and foremost about what we see happening on screen, not about the lines that are spoken, as clever as they might be! The general agreement in screenwriting is simple: the more lines of dialogue in a script, the least visual it actually might be.

What's more atrocious than a page filled with thick paragraphs of description in a script? Definitely a page packed with infinite lines of dialogue!

*Remember: a script is not a stage or a radio play. The fundamental talent of a screenwriter lies in their ability to express sophisticated and complicated actions, filled with subtext and deep internal emotions, **visually**! That means, with pictures.*

And to do so, the easiest way for a lot of people is to get the characters to just… utter those deep feelings on screen, throw out their guts orally on the poor viewer.

How more visual could you be, right? We do actually see the characters talk…

*Well, not really! "**People talking on screen" is not the most visual picture you can come up with. Eisenstein,** the father of editing, used to appropriately mock the inanity of dialogue: "**How cheap it is to hear words and watch mouths move…**" You get the same by simply filming a play, and last time I checked, that's not a movie.*

Unfortunately, that's what beginners and the less talented screenwriters would actually do, instead of creating the appropriate actions and scenes that would express the desired emotions, without dialogue!

Which, I agree, is so darn difficult…

And that's how they end up with long pages filled with lines after lines of dialogue without actions.

Which, I agree again, is so much darn easier.

Technically, you should consider creating a line of dialogue only when you have exhausted all efforts to convey your idea by visual means. It's your last resort, as it were… And even in that case, try to use the least amount of words possible, hoping that a combination of minimal words and more actions would still express the idea in a powerful visual way.

Let's go back to Richard as he tries to settle into his shabby hotel room:

```
================================================================

INT. HOTEL ROOM — NIGHT

Cold, cheap…

Richard THROWS his suitcase on the tiny bed, rushes to the
air conditioner.

It comes to life as he PUSHES the ON button, for maybe two
seconds. Then SPUTTERS, COUGHS and wilts down in a whirl of
SCREECHING sounds.

                    RICHARD
          Damn it! How in the world am I
          supposed to sleep tonight with
          hundred and four degrees outside!

He OPENS the window, deeply BREATHES IN, hoping for a
breeze.

                    RICHARD
          Aaarrgh! Not a single breeze!

He violently CLOSES the window. The glass BREAKS.

================================================================
```

Boring, redundant and filled with superfluous lines!

Here is how to get a more visual and exciting scene, without even one line of dialogue:

```
================================================================

INT. HOTEL ROOM — NIGHT

Cold, cheap…

Richard, soaked in sweat, THROWS his suitcase on the tiny
bed, rushes to the air conditioner.

It comes to life as he PUSHES the ON button, for maybe two
seconds. Then SPUTTERS, COUGHS and wilts down in a whirl of
SCREECHING sounds.

Richard SIGHS: This is not going to be a good night…

He OPENS the window, hoping for a breeze.

Then violently CLOSES it. The glass BREAKS.

================================================================
```

In a sense, screenwriters have definitely mixed feelings when using dialogue: It's a part of life, people do talk and express themselves mostly with words, and so it should be used to make the characters more believable.

However, because we deal with this particular medium for which visualization is essential, the tendency is to employ as little dialogue as possible, hoping to convey most of your ideas visually.

What a Dilemma!

That's why for the purists, resorting to dialogue is tantamount a… failure to find visual expressions for their ideas! And so they feel very distressed whenever they give a line to their characters.

How extreme is that? Not very… especially if you have to read pages and pages of boring, tasteless, insipid and contrived dialogue!

So, use your words sparingly! Forget about dialogue as you create your scenes. You should focus first and foremost on your visuals: Try your best to express ideas, feelings and thoughts visually, meaning through action.

But when you hit that proverbial wall, and you can't find a way to express, say… that fleeting feeling between characters in love but tortured with suspicion, then use a few words, as little as possible to convey the delicate moment. And quickly get back to your visuals!

In short, don't ever get swayed by the seduction of dialogue. It seems so innocuous, so easy, so real… And before you know it, there goes a whole page of inane lines!

Paddy Chayevsky, the famed writer of **Network** and **Being There,** had no hesitation when it came to his own lines: **"Dialogue comes because I know what I want my characters to say. I envision the scene - and the dialogue comes out of that. Then I rewrite it. Then I cut it. Then I refine it until I get the scene as precise as I can get it."**

28/ Dialogue and Characters

Think about one simple fact: with six billion people on this planet, you would be hard pressed to find two people that look the same, or talk the same, for that matter. True, we all apparently have somewhere a double that suspiciously looks like us. Just like most of us, I haven't found mine yet… But try to find two people who speak exactly the same, using the same language within the same culture, with the same regionalism, slang, jargon and even accent!

So, how come that in most of the scripts that vie for attention on the market, the majority of the characters hopelessly speak in the same exact manner? If a middle age male meatpacker, an older female aristocrat, an early teens student and a very famous writer inadvertently were to meet and somehow describe an accident they witnessed on their way home, I would have difficulties accepting the fact that they would all deliver the same exact lines of dialogue.

You get my point by now: dialogue is as unique to a character as any of the traits, quirks, habits, slang, jargon, accent or other idiosyncrasies that you give them.

Cathy Rabin, Vice President at **Meg Ryan's** company, **Fandango Films,** is definitely clear about this issue: **"Dialogue should be organic to the character. Each**

character should have a distinctive voice, and while snappy patter and 'bon mots' are fun and appreciated, one has to be careful not to allow glibness to take precedence."

*And **Michael Serafin**, another Hollywood story analyst, admits: "A lot of writers will write all their characters exactly the same. Sometimes I can't even tell which character is the male and which is the female by reading the dialogue. Interchangeability in dialogue can do great damage to a script."*

In a sense, dialogue is part of the DNA of a given character you create! You should not have in a script two characters that have the same dialogue. Unfortunately, most beginners end up with exactly that: all characters speaking in the same exact way, which usually ends up being the way the very screenwriter speaks in real life…

Now how surprising is that?

Dialogue has to be polished and refined like jewels for every single character and every single line, so that not only is it unique to that character, but it also has to ring right and feel real. Well-written scripts will have dialogue that's so well crafted and so unique to the characters that after a few pages, I am able to know who speaks even if I didn't read the character slug!

*By now you see why dialogue is so difficult to write, and why very few writers are talented when it comes to choosing the correct lines for their characters. You also understand how easy it is for beginners to fall into what is known as the **"dialogue trap"** where all we see are pages of inane lines that emulate real life conversations.*

*Here is how **Daryl Ponicsan**, the famed writer of **The Last Detail, Taps, Nuts** and **Random Hearts**, sees the issue: "A script should be so rooted in reality that you're not conscious that someone has written it. If you come out of a movie saying 'What a great dialogue,' the movie didn't work well. The dialogue that actors do best is basically non-dialogue that is believable and rooted solely in behavior. Otherwise it calls too much attention to the writer."*

29/ Dialogue Directions/Parentheticals/Personal Directions

Dialogue Directions, or **Parentheticals**, also known as **Wrylies** in Hollywood parlance, are specific instructions intended for a speaking character, informing the reader about **how**, **to whom** or **what** kind of action is taken as that particular line is actually delivered.

Dialogue directions are usually very short, no more than two or three words! If longer, then you should simply write them as straight directions.

Parentheticals are indicated as follows:

One space under the name of the character,

5 spaces to the left, which is **2 inches** from the left margin,

And in **parentheses!**

Here is how it should look like:

```
========================================================

                    RICHARD
                   (Angrily)
         Please, try to understand me…

========================================================
```

Parentheticals are preferably written in the form of an adverb: **angrily, sheepishly, dryly, happily…** But even simple action verbs could be used: **shouting, mumbling** or **whispering.** They also indicate to whom the character is talking. Here are a few other examples for a correct use of parentheticals:

(To Jennifer)
(Back to Caroline)
(Staring at him)

As a rule, try to not overuse dialogue directions, particularly when your intent is to simply replace descriptions. How easy it is to throw a prenthetical under each speaking character and avoid descriptions alltogether! But that's not the way it is intended. Remember that directors and especially actors hate parentheticals: You are clearly meddling with their jobs!

The best advice is to use dialogue directions when a line is actually delivered in a surprisingly different way than the reader would otherwise understand; which would clearly confuse the reader. You expect Richard to shout when he actually whispers. You believe this line is meant to appease things between the two characters, when in fact it pushes Richard to explode. You think maybe Richard is romancing Jennifer, when, down deep, he is enraged.

Here is a good use of a parenthetical:

```
================================================================

                    RICHARD
                 (Shouting)
        But hell, I love you so much!

================================================================
```

Here is a redundant use of parentheticals:

```
================================================================

                    RICHARD
                 (Happily)
        That was the happiest day of my
        entire life.

================================================================
```

Another good use of parentheticals is when a line is addressed to someone we couldn't clearly identify in a crowd. Richard talks to Mary, but this particular line goes to Jim, who is standing behind him. A parenthetical could then be legitimately used.

```
============================================================
                      RICHARD
          Not to offend you, but I am not
          very hungry.
                    (To Jim)
          We should get going, man!

============================================================
```

Dialogue directions are also used when a character is talking on the phone and we want to make sure the viewer knows exactly that, as opposed to the character talking to someone else:

```
============================================================


                      RICHARD
                  (On the phone)
          Can I call you at this number?

============================================================
```

30/ Of Beats and Pauses

*I guess, everyone knows what a pause is. A beat on the other hand is borrowed directly from poetry or music. The dictionary defines beat as "**a rhythmic stress in poetry or music, a single stroke or pulsation**"… I am still wondering what the connection with screenwriting is! I suspect that beat is used interchangeably for pause.*

*Whether beat or pause, it is very problematic when screenwriters fill their lines with parentheticals indicating **pauses** and **beats,** trying to inform the viewer* *how that particular line is actually delivered, with all its silences and pauses and moments of hesitation.*

Nice try!

Look at it this way: There is nothing more egregious than a screenwriter telling a director or an actor how they should deliver a speech or when they should make a pause!

In terms of writing, it's technically the same wrong approach and the same erroneous thought process as with the lengthy detailed directions we discussed earlier.

So, forget about pauses and beats! If needed, actors will pause, insert a beat or express uncertainty in their own way, in agreement with the director and no matter what you might write in your parenthetical.

The only situation I can think of where a pause or a beat could be appropriately used is when a character is conversing with someone on the phone in a one-sided way: The character we actually see is listening, while the person on the other end of the line is talking.

Here is how it might look:

```
================================================================

                         RICHARD
                    (On the phone)
              Can I call you at this number?
                      (Pause)
              What do you mean you don't know the
              number?
                      (Pause)
              Oh, a phone booth. What happened to
              our cell phone?

================================================================
```

31/ Talking Between Pages

When a long dialogue (and again dialogue should never be long!) jumps between pages, a few rules apply:

If possible, try to end your page with a complete line so that you don't inconvenience the reader.

If not, then at the bottom of the unfinished dialogue, right at the center, write:

(MORE)

*In **parentheses** and **uppercase**!*

On the following page, start again at the top with the character slug of the talking character, and add beside it:

(CONT'D)

*Again, in **parentheses** and **uppercase**! Here is Richard, still trying to make his case:*

```
================================================================


                    RICHARD
                  (Angrily)
         Please, try to understand me…
                    (MORE)


-------------------------Next Page-------------------------

                                                  15.


                    RICHARD (CONT'D)
         I have to take this job!


================================================================
```

By the way, never, ever end a page with a character slug dangling alone without an actual line.

```
================================================================

                    RICHARD

----------------------Next Page------------------------

                                                    15.

            (Angrily)
        Please, try to understand me… I have
        to take this job!


================================================================
```

If you inadvertently find yourself without room for even one line of dialogue after writing the character slug, your best choice will be to move the whole dialogue with the character slug to the next page.

A final warning though: whatever software you use to write your opus might automatically and unfortunately add to your characters' slugs the following:

(CONT'D)

Or

(Cont'd)

This happens in special situations such as when your character stops talking, does some kind of action, and then resumes their dialogue. Which is definitely a very outdated way of writing that simply adds more words on the page.

*Turn off that feature from your "**Preferences**" and, as explained above, (CONT'D) or (Cont'd) should be used only when a dialogue is split between two pages.*

*A **final note:** most professional screenwriting software programs will automatically adjust dialogue between pages as well as any other kind of space issue as you move from one page to the next. They will even re-format your entire script appropriately when you make any changes that affect its length.*

CHAPTER SIX

WHAT ELSE COULD YOU HEAR

"Be professional: do not conceal in the off-camera directions important information the audience need to know."

Linda Stuart
Story Analyst

32/ Sounds and Sound Effects

*Always **capitalize** words or verbs that describe or suggest a sound, a sound effect or any strong audio component such as:*

SLAM
SHOOT
RING
BELL,
EXPLODE
BRAKE
SMASH
SHOUT

It helps to create the mood and it makes the script page visually more appealing and the reading easier. It mostly helps the production process as technicians get an idea of what to expect in terms of sound and sound effects.

That said, I have to admit that the implementation of this rule tends to confuse students faced with sometimes very extensive choices. Here is an example:

===

Exasperated, Jennifer heads towards the door when the bell rings.

===

Do we capitalize "bell", or "rings", or both?

Simple: If you have a verb that conveys the nature of the sound, capitalize it! In this case, "rings" is best:

===

Exasperated, Jennifer heads towards the door when the bell RINGS.

===

On the other hand, if you lack a verb, capitalize the noun that best conveys the nature of the sound. In the following case, "bell" is the best-suited noun to use:

===

Exasperated, Jennifer heads towards the door when the BELL is heard.

===

*But whatever the case, **NEVER CAPITALIZE** an adjective or an adverb that qualifies the sound we hear.*

*So **AVOID** the following:*

===

Exasperated, Jennifer heads towards the door when the bell RINGS INSISTENTLY.

Then, out of nowhere, LOUD KNOCKS seem to come through the walls, followed by TORTURED WAILS and HORRIFYING HOWLS…

===

*A caveat however about capitalizing the sound effects: **DO NOT** be surprised if you read a current script with absolutely no sound capitalization whatsoever. There is lately a tendency in lazy Hollywood to simplify the writing and to omit any mention of sound. It's the "who cares?" attitude promoted again by writers who have never done any kind of actual production. I do believe that capitalizing verbs or nouns that convey a sound makes for a much better reading while effectively helping the production process.*

*So, **CAPITALIZE YOUR SOUNDS!***

*Thinking of it, the use of the word "**sound**" is also very problematic in a screenplay. Students have this tendency to actually overuse it to convey… well, the sound!*

Here is how it could become obnoxious:

```
================================================================

Exasperated, Jennifer heads towards the door when the SOUND
of the doorbell is heard.

Then, out of nowhere, the SOUND of loud knocks comes
through the walls, followed by the SOUND of tortured wails
and horrifying howls… The SOUND of her loud heartbeat joins
the appalling cacophony.

================================================================
```

Apart from the obvious redundancy, you realize how we might end up with one single word, capitalized again and again ad nauseam: SOUND! And I have seen this countless times, even in professional scripts.

*Actually, when describing sounds, you should avoid as much as possible the word **sound** altogether. There are a thousand verbs that could easily and more efficiently convey the idea of the particular sound you have in mind. Unless you are trying to express the indefinite nature of a mysterious sound, which is difficult to describe and hard to fathom…*

Here is again Jennifer, still facing the ominous and unfathomable sounds in her room.

```
================================================================

Exasperated, Jennifer heads towards the door when a
mysterious SOUND slowly starts. It feels like KNOCKING,
loud, obnoxious and enervating, coming in successive
rhythmic waves through the walls, but which one?

================================================================
```

33/ Diegetic and Non-diegetic Sounds

A reputable dictionary defines **Diegesis** as the Greek word for "recounted story" or simply, storytelling. A film diegesis refers to the total world of the story's action and sounds.

From that perspective, two kinds of sounds and sound effects are available to a screenwriter:

Diegetic Sound, or **Actual Sound** exists when the source of a particular sound is either clearly visible on screen or considered to be present through the introduced action. This could be the voice of the characters, the sounds made by objects on screen or in the scene, such as a radio or TV, or the music coming from instruments in the actual location. Diegetic sound can be either **on screen** or **off screen**, depending on whether its source is within the actual scene or in its vicinity.

Non-Diegetic Sound or **Commentary Sound** refers to a sound whose source is not visible on the screen and not implied to be present in the action such as a narrator's comments, sound effects that are non-existent on screen or its vicinity but added for dramatic effect, or a musical score added for emotional effect. Non-diegetic sounds come from a source outside the story space. A good example would be an omniscient narrator that we never see on screen.

Obviously, the distinction between diegetic and non-diegetic sound is essential for the reader to understand the story and the intricacies of the sounds effects on screen, or off screen. Which is even more essential for the technicians during production and post-production.

Here is how all this is designed, then indicated in the script.

34/ Dialogue Extensions

A **dialogue extension** generally informs the reader about a particular sound or voice, diegetic or non-diegetic, and about its provenance in relation to the scene we are actually watching.

*Dialogue extensions usually follow a character's name, they are always **capitalized**, and they are always written in **parentheses**! Luckily, there are not too many of them…*

*If your scene is taking place in a kitchen, and Richard is talking to Jennifer who is on the first floor, and we don't actually see Jennifer, then all her lines should automatically be labeled **off screen**, written:*

(O.S.)

Right beside the character's name!

*However, if Jennifer at some point enters the kitchen, her dialogue obviously becomes on-screen as we see her, which means **NO** (O.S.) should be added to her lines anymore.*

*But please, **DO NOT** use OFF-CAMERA instead of OFF-SCREEN. This, again, was invented by disgruntled writers and abbreviated (O.C.). Remember: There is no camera and there is nothing inside it or… outside of it for that matter. It's all about what we see on screen, which is what you describe. OFF-CAMERA is simply an oxymoron.*

To summarize: writing a character slug without any dialogue extension automatically means that we see the character talking on screen!

Speaking of which, here is a very special case I need to direct your attention to, as students get consistently confused when addressing it:

*When two, three or more characters speak in the same setting, **DON'T EVER** jump from off screen to on screen based on how you foresee the scene visually evolving. If all characters are present in the scene you just labeled, then for all intents and purposes they are all considered to be on screen at any given time even if the emphasis is on the one who is not talking.*

However, if one of them leaves, we know what to do then.

*This is what I have in mind and what you should always **AVOID**:*

```
================================================================
```

Surprised, Richard watches as she quickly stands up.

                    JENNIFER (O.S)
          This is ridiculous!
                    (grabs a Kleenex)
          I don't want to talk about…

Overwhelmed with tears, she walks out of the kitchen.

                    RICHARD (O.S.)
          Wait a second, we need to talk about
          this right now!

She SLAMS the door, heads towards the first floor, still
SHOUTING.

                    JENNIFER (O.S.)
          I don't want this marriage! Just leave
          me alone.

Then, nothing! Just her SOBS, intermittent and fading…

```
================================================================
```


Here is the problem: In the first two lines, you are evidently making directorial decisions such as whom I see on screen and who is currently off screen.

Jennifer says: "This is ridiculous" off screen, which can only mean that I am actually seeing Richard and his reaction as she talks.

When she grabs the Kleenex, I evidently see her as she says: "I don't want to talk about…"

And when Richard finally responds, we are definitely focused on Jennifer who is just leaving, thus Richard is not seen on screen.

If these are not directorial decisions, I don't know what directorial decisions are anymore!

Here is how it should be correctly written:

```
================================================================

Surprised, Richard watches as she stands up, grabs a
Kleenex.

                         JENNIFER
                This is ridiculous! I don't want to
                talk about…

Overwhelmed with tears, she walks out of the kitchen.

                         RICHARD
                Wait a second, we need to talk about
                this right now!

She SLAMS the door. Her STEPS seem to head towards the
first floor as she SHOUTS.

                       JENNIFER (O.S.)
                I don't want this marriage! Just leave
                me alone.

Then, nothing! Just her SOBS, intermittent and fading…

================================================================
```

On the other hand, a **Voice-Over**, written:

(V.O.)

is simply the mechanical transmission of an off-screen voice. The person, who speaks, is not physically present, neither on screen nor in the immediate vicinity. Generally, it's a voice coming from some electric or electronic communication device such as a telephone, a P.A. system, an amplifier, an answering machine or a narrator's voice. A voice-over is most definitely a non-diegetic sound!

Sometimes the characters might be present and even visible on screen, but we do not actually see them mouthing any words: We hear their thoughts or comments over the scene as they think out loud… You know the kind of comments that characters unabashedly share with us mortal viewers…

In such a case, the (V.O.) is very appropriate.

Here is Jennifer squaring off with Richard in a different manner:

===

                        JENNIFER
          I don't want to talk about it.

                        RICHARD
          Wait a second, we need to talk about
          this right now!

Overwhelmed with tears, Jennifer walks out of the kitchen.

She SLAMS the door, heads towards the first floor, still
SHOUTING.

                        JENNIFER (O.S.)
          I don't want this marriage! Just leave
          me alone.

Then, nothing! Just her SOBS, intermittent and fading…

Richard slowly gathers his files, moves towards the door.

                        RICHARD (V.O.)
          That was the very first time we ever
          fought. She seemed literally in a world
          of her own…

===

The dialogue extensions indicated above are self-explanatory. However, when a character speaks from a computer monitor, a television screen or any other sound, video or film device, you can either use the (V.O.) and explain in the preceding directions the provenance of the particular line, or simply use a dialogue extension that directly indicates the origin of the dialogue, such as:

                        (ON TV)

(ON SCREEN)

(ON CELL PHONE)

(ON COMPUTER)

(FROM RADIO)

(FROM P.A. SYSTEM)

Here is the case when you describe the provenance of the dialogue with a (V.O.):

```
================================================================

Just as Richard moves towards the door, the TV suddenly
COMES ON, loud and obnoxious.

The anchor, a woman with a husky voice, SHOUTS at the
world, threatening weather predictions.

                        ANCHOR (V.O.)
             …I wouldn't recommend any driving on
             Highway 94 between Monticello and
             St. Cloud. Folks, this is a serious
             storm…

Richard looks around for a remote to kill the deafening
voice.

================================================================
```


And here is the case when you describe the provenance of the line in the dialogue extension:

```
================================================================

Just as Richard moves towards the door, the TV suddenly
COMES ON, loud and obnoxious.

                        ANCHOR (ON TV)
```

> …I wouldn't recommend any driving on
> Highway 94 between Monticello and
> St. Cloud. Folks, this is a serious
> storm…

Richard looks around for a remote to kill the threatening voice.

===

And in case you decide to feature in your script that undefined and threatening voice from your favorite scary movie, mysteriously coming from nowhere, simply use:

> (VOICE)

as a character slug and treat it like any other speaking part from there on.

*Finally, **DO NOT** slug a recorded voice from an answering machine, a P.R. system or a radio. Those are sound devices that don't really talk. Usually, a voice belongs hopefully to a living character, and it happens to come through these devices.*

So, simply use the Voice-over. Here is an example:

===

Richard feverishly GATHERS his files, moves towards the blinking answering machine. He PUSHES the PLAY button while STUFFING more documents in his attaché-case.

Jennifer's VOICE playfully BURSTS into the room.

> JENNIFER (V.O.)
> Hi! We decided to tour the blue planet,
> so no one is around. But if it's
> urgent, you know what to do with the
> answering machine… Bye!

The machine BEEPS, his own VOICE follows, happy but somehow disappointed.

                    RICHARD (V.O)
          Hi Jenny! I… I got the job! It's gonna
          be great. I am on my way to your place
          right now… We need, well… we should…
          OK, we will talk. Love ya!

Then a CLICK!

Almost instantaneously Richard SMACKS the STOP button.

==

35/ Music

Diegetic music and any kind of specific music from a specific singer or composer playing on screen call for **capitalization** *as well, such as:*

OPERA, SWING, JAZZ, PIANO, TECHNO MUSIC, BEETHOVEN, MOZART, OSCAR PETERSON, MAHLER'S FIRST SYMPHONY, REQUIEM, MENDELSSOHN'S THIRD CONCERTO, *etc.*

Here is an example:

==

Exasperated, Jennifer WALKS OUT, heads towards the first floor.

Suddenly, out of nowhere, a maddening TECHNO MUSIC fills the house.

==

The operating rule in music is to **AVOID** *indicating any non-diegetic musical score in your directions for the same obvious reasons we already discussed many times before: the director will be the one making that kind of creative decision!*

*This, for instance, should **NEVER EVER** appear in your script:*

```
================================================================

Exasperated, Jennifer WALKS OUT, heads towards the first
floor. John is unable to react as he hears her
SLAM the doors and SWEAR at him from a room upstairs.

Slowly, the VIOLINS start a sad melody. The WINDS join in,
adding uncertainty and mystery. Finally, a TRUMPET SHOUTS
dissonantly, a long and ominous cry of the heart!

================================================================
```

You see the point?

It's not your job as a writer to give any indication about the future score of the movie, even if you were the likely musician who will later write it!

Scores are traditionally added much later to the edited movie, in specific moments, for specific directing effects, in order to create a particular set of emotions. What if the director decided not to add any music at the very moment you suggested your strings should crescendo and your winds follow suit? What if your director wanted just plain silence?

*So, don't make a fool of yourself and follow the simple rule: the only kind of music you are allowed to add in your script is the one that is part of the action in a scene, known as **Prop Music**, **Diegetic Music** or **Actual Music**: A radio in the location, a TV or a CD playing some kind of music that we hear, a far away music from some open device in the street or from the neighbors at two in the morning, or maybe someone directly playing or rehearsing an instrument in your very scene. That should definitely be indicated in a script!*

Here is how you could correctly write, and yet never dream of that Oscar:

===

Exasperated, Jennifer WALKS OUT, her STEPS seem to head toward the first floor. John is unable to react when she SLAMS the doors and is vaguely heard SWEARING at him from a room upstairs.

He ponders his next move for a moment, OPENS the closet, grabs his violin.

It takes him a moment before any music comes out. Then, more assertive, he starts a sad MELODY.

He closes his eyes, seemingly lost in a world of sorrow.

It is sweet and sad. Tears slowly roll down his cheeks.

Suddenly, a dissonant NOTE ERUPTS, then ANOTHER, finally a long ONE, as if an ominous cry of the heart.

Out of nowhere, a maddening TECHNO MUSIC fills the house. John violently THROWS the violin away.

===

CHAPTER SEVEN

<u>DIALOGUE CONSIDERATIONS</u>

"We really respond to great dialogue. If the dialogue is right on - if it's true to character and does more than just advance the plot - we'll tend to be enthusiastic about the writer."

Gregory Avellone
Tig Productions
Kevin Costner's company

36/ Subtitles, Foreign Language, Accent, Dialect and More

In case your character speaks a **foreign language**, avoid writing both the foreign language and the English simultaneously or side by side. It becomes confusing, redundant and definitely long.

Here are the best solutions to choose from for such particular cases:

a. Write the line directly in the foreign language, but with **quotes** so that the reader realizes it actually is spoken in a different language:

===

                            RODRIGO
                    "Donde es su padre?"

===

b. Write the line directly in English, without the quotes, but indicate in a parenthetical the particular language used:

===

                            RODRIGO
                          (in Italian)
                      Where is your father?

===

c. Write your line in English or in whatever other language, without quotes, but explain it to the viewer in your directions.

```
================================================================
```

ALBERT, a mid-twenties macho heartthrob with superficial
manners creeps into the kitchen. He speaks FRENCH, with a
distinct Southern accent.

                    ALBERT
          Où est ton père?


```
================================================================
```

    d. *Finally, you might decide to use English on-screen*
subtitles, which certainly will help the viewer
understand the lines. In such a case, just describe
the process in your directions as simply and as
succinctly as possible:


```
================================================================
```

SELIM, a mid-twenties macho heartthrob with superficial
manners, creeps into the kitchen. He speaks BERBER with a
distinct North African accent.

The following lines are in BERBER with ENGLISH SUBTITLES.

                    SELIM
          Where is your father?

                    FATIMA
          Still at the hospital… Why do you
          care suddenly?

                    SELIM
          I like the man. He has always been
          like a father to me.

                    FATIMA
          Amazing what a little cash can do…


```
================================================================
```

*As a general rule you should **AVOID** trying to emulate phonetically any dialect, accent, jargon, Southern drawl or other accents, such as the funky Minnesota "Yaaa's" and other "You Betchyaa's…"*

***AVOID**, in particular, writing phonetically how a character stutters! That's a definite killer!*

```
================================================================

GIORGIO, a mid-twenties macho heartthrob with superficial
manners, creeps into the kitchen. He speaks with a painful
stutter.

                        GIORGIO
                      (stuttering)
             Whe… whe… where i… i… i…uh… is yo… yo…
             y… your… father?

                        MARTHA
             Still at the hospital… What do you
             care all of a sudden?

Phil stops preparing his sandwich at the counter.

                         PHIL
                       (tired)
             I better be goin… I'll be eatin mi
             sandwich in the thoyd flawh cafeteria,
             if you know what I mean…


================================================================
```

Literally painful to even read!

Phonetically written speeches are hard to understand and hard to follow for more than one line. It will not take long before they throw your script in the garbage!

What to do? Again, simplicity! Just indicate in your directions or in a parenthetical that the given character speaks with a delightful accent, a forgotten dialect, a heavy southern drawl, a funny Mid-western accent or a painful stutter.

==

SELIM, a mid-twenties macho heartthrob with superficial
manners, creeps into the kitchen. He speaks BERBER, with a
distinct NORTH AFRICAN accent.

                        SELIM
              Where is your father?

                        FATIMA
                  (stuttering)
              Still at the hospital… What do you
              fucking care all of a sudden?

George stops preparing his sandwich at the counter.

                        GEORGE
                  (heavy Southern drawl)
              I better be going. I'll be eating
              my sandwich in the third floor cafeteria,
              if you know what I mean…

==

*The reason, again: it is not your job to figure out
how that particular character is going to use the heavy
Mid-western accent and how it is really going to sound. If
needed, a **Dialogue Director** will be brought to the set to
teach and train the actors so that they correctly pronounce
whatever jargon, accent, slang, and dialect or stutter you
requested in your directions.*

*So, just indicate your choice, the dialogue directors
will do the rest and believe me, they are paid very well to
do just that!*

37/ *Double Dashes and Ellipses*

*Double dashes and ellipses have been a constant
headache for beginning and experienced screenwriters alike.
Often, when characters converse, someone or something might
interrupt them. A **double-dash** is then needed after whatever
word or syllable they were stopped at:*

--

If they resume their lines in mid-sentence despite the interruption, then you should also use the double-dash before their words.

*Now if they stop in mid-sentence for a thoughtful moment, if their line dribbles away, overcome by emotion, indecision or boredom, or if we move slowly into a fantasy, a flashback, a vision or a dream, then we need an **ellipsis:***

...

Here is how it looks:

```
================================================================

                         JENNIFER
              I don't want to talk about it! I--

                          RICHARD
              Wait a second! We need to sort this
              out right--

                         JENNIFER
              --don't want this marriage!

Overwhelmed with tears, Jennifer walks out of the kitchen.

Somewhere in the house a door is SLAMMED, followed by an
exhausted SHOUT.

                      JENNIFER(O.S.)
              Just leave me alone! I…

Then nothing! Just her SOBS, intermittent and fading.

================================================================
```

*By the way, as we discussed earlier, **DO NOT** use ellipses to indicate pauses! Whenever a character pauses as they speak or during an action, describe it in a direction*

*or in a parenthetical, as simply as possible. Here is a
direction in lieu of a pause:*

```
================================================================
```

Richard thinks for a moment, looks intently at Jennifer,
as if unable to believe what she just said.

```
================================================================
```

38/ *Simultaneous Dialogue*

*This is when you decide, for whatever reason, to have
certain conversations occur simultaneously, whether by
design or just by sheer chance. Here is what you could
still encounter in many a smart screenplay, written by
renowned screenwriters.*

AVOID *at all costs!*

```
================================================================
```

EXT./INT. PARK/JANE'S KITCHEN — DAY

Richard and Jane continue their heated conversation over
the phone as Jane prepares her salad in the kitchen and
Richard walks aimlessly through the park, puffing on his
hand-rolled cigarette.

RICHARD	JANE
I can't do it right now!	But you promised, you promised to be here for her…

RICHARD	JANE
(Shouting)	(Hysterical)
I know I did! But something came up… I need to make a living you know--	And I need to take care of a child that hasn't seen her father for days… Shit!

Jane suddenly cuts herself with the oversized knife. Blood!
Lots of it, everywhere…

```
================================================================
```

Confusing, very difficult to read, poorly presented, aesthetically obnoxious, and ultimately nauseating…

Here are two ways how to best deal with such extreme cases:

a. Write a fragment of the first character's lines, use the double dashes (--) to interrupt the dialogue, write the next character's line and add in parentheticals either:

(Simultaneously)

Or

(Overlapping)

Then return to your first character's line in mid-sentence and have them interrupted again, etc.

b. Or simply write your lines and add to them from time to time either:

(Simultaneously)

Or

(Overlapping)

Here is how Richard and Jane could continue their fight over the phone, simultaneously shouting at each other:

==

EXT./INT. PARK/JANE'S KITCHEN — DAY

Richard and Jane continue their heated conversation over
the phone as Jane prepares her salad in the kitchen and
Richard walks aimlessly through the park, puffing on his
hand-rolled cigarette.

                    RICHARD
          I just can't do it right now!

                    JANE
               (Shouting)
          But you promised, you promised to be
          here for her--

                    RICHARD
               (Overlapping)
          I know I did! But something came up… I
          need to make a living you know--

                    JANE
               (Simultaneously)
          And I need to take care of a child
          that hasn't seen her father all day
          long… Shit! Shit! Shit!

Jane suddenly cuts herself with the oversized knife. Blood!
Lots of it, everywhere…

Unaware, Richard continues to SHOUT over the phone, irate.

                    RICHARD
          Well you're gonna have to choose
          between that kind of father and
          simply no father… And no husband!

==

39/ Numbering and Dialogue

*If you happen to have numbers in your dialogue, you
should clearly spell them so that we know how you want them
pronounced. It has to do with the character traits and
their way of expressing things.*

*Here is what you should **AVOID**:*

```
================================================================
Richard feverishly gathers his files, moves towards the
blinking answering machine.

He PUSHES the PLAY button while STUFFING more documents in
his attaché. Jennifer's VOICE playfully BURSTS out.

                    JENNIFER (V.O.)
          Hi! I decided to tour the blue planet,
          so no one is around. But if it's urgent,
          call me on my cell: 612-555-5555. Bye!

================================================================
```

What exactly are we supposed to read when she gives her phone number?

Six-one-two, five-five-five, five-five, five-five,

Or

Six-one-two, five fifty-five, fifty-five, fifty-five,

Or

Six Hundred and Twelve, five hundred fifty-five, Five Thousand Five Hundred and Fifty-Five,

Or

Six Hundred and Twelve, five-five-five, fifty-five, fifty-five,

Or…

You realize the choices! And each one qualifies your character differently.

Just clearly spell your choice in writing, and you will make everybody's life easier while revealing more about your character and his/her unique traits.

40/ Singing and Reciting in Dialogue

If your character happens to be reciting a poem or singing a song, you will convey that best when using **quotation marks** *and writing your poem or song line over line. Then indicate into parentheticals that your character is actually*

                 (reciting)

Or

                 (singing)

Here is how it should look if you decide to get into a stupid musical like this one:

```
================================================================

Richard feverishly gathers his files, moves towards the
blinking answering machine. He PUSHES the PLAY button while
STUFFING more documents in his attaché. Jennifer's VOICE
playfully BURSTS at his face.

                    JENNIFER (V.O.)
                  (singing)
          "Hello… Hello… Hello…!
          Wherever you are bound
          No one is really around.
          But here is the machine,
          And in case of emergency,
          Suit yourself with leniency,
          Call my cell phone,
          I will happily quit my throne,
          Promptly respond to your quest
          And as usual do my best!"

A quirky TONE follows the voice, but nothing else.

Richard PUSHES the STOP button and seems suddenly lost in
deep meditation.

================================================================
```

CHAPTER EIGHT

IT'S DONE... WHAT NOW?

Two development execs meet in a hallway.
One says, "Hey, what's cooking?"
The second one, extremely excited, replies,
"I just bought this script.
It's the most perfect piece of writing I've ever seen.
Characters, story, EVERYTHING about it is A-number-one.
Academy award time."
"Fantastic," says the first.
"So when do you go into production?"
"As soon as I get the rewrite."

Reported by
Charles Deemer

41/ So You Really Think It Is Done?

Critical question as it were, when you remember the curmudgeonly **Ernest Hemingway** lament: **The first draft of anything is shit.**" Then again, nothing is more ironically tragic than the fate of those who think they know, when they actually don't know what they… simply don't know!

Daryl Ponicsan, the writer of **Nuts**, **Taps**, **School Ties** and **Angel Hearts** is very hesitant when it comes to really finishing a script: **"I don't think you should let a script go before it's ready. That is a failing for a lot of writers. You have to wait until you are really convinced that you've got something special. And if you truly have something special, there will be no problem getting anyone to read it."**

The number of professionally "unfinished" scripts producers receive on a daily basis is staggering. And right at the very beginning, you will find incorrect elements that will simply invite the executive to throw the darn thing in the garbage!

Martha Browning, the story analyst for **Morgan Creek**, knows a lot about scripts deemed "ready" for consideration: **"It's almost as if these people haven't read their scripts before they send them out. I've read scripts that would need to give the audience a chart to take into the theater with them. I've said in my coverage that if the audience didn't have a blueprint and a family tree they would never know what was going on."**

After you put FADE OUT at the end of your umpteenth script, you should ask yourself at least the following basic questions:

Is it correctly formatted?
Is it really polished?
Has it been rewritten enough times to showcase your material in the best possible light?
And very importantly, has it been thoroughly edited?

I am here talking about the very basics: misspellings, typos, overused punctuation, grammar, formatting, page numbers, slug-lines, slug extensions, character extensions and the like…

Here is what should be carefully considered before you send out that script to a studio or a producer:

42/ Punctuation and Grammar

Ladies and Gentlemen, basic grammar rules still apply when you are writing your script, including punctuation. And readers hate mistakes more than anybody else. Look at it this way: They are really looking for any reason to not read your script.

Articles and pronouns like "a", "the", "an", "her", "his", cannot be dropped, for any reason. Just try to make sense of the following actions:

```
================================================================


Man opens door, sees mailman, closes door quickly. Man runs
to safe, quickly opens it, grabs wads of money.

Man stuffs money in bag, opens window, jumps into street.


================================================================
```

Positively ridiculous and obnoxious! They most likely will help a reader close your script as fast as they can. We still might understand the actions, but it makes for a miserable reading experience, and that experience is important for you to stay in the game.

NEVER *start a scene with a pronoun, even if your character is alone in the scene. Directions such as:* **He enters, they walk, she runs** *or any other comparable action at the beginning of a scene are simply not acceptable.*

*Then, it is imperative that you **AVOID** the usual misspellings that most would-be screenwriters seem to relish.*

Just for fun, here is a list of the most common confusions I've seen in students' works, but also, believe it or not, in some of the most respectable scripts as well:

Its *and* **It's**
Your *and* **You're**
There, Their *and* **They're**
Then *and* **Than**
Tale *and* **Tail**
Pack *and* **Pact**
Desert *and* **Dessert**
Meat *and* **Meet**
Let's *and* **Lets**
Lay *and* **Lie**
Affect *and* **Effect**
Two, Too *and* **To**
Our *and* **Are**
Whose *and* **Who's**
You Would Of *and* **You Would've**
Principal *and* **Principle**
A Boyfriend of Hers *and* **A Boyfriend of Her's**

Here is an excerpt, loaded with wisdom and sagacity, ready to definitely catapult you to the Academy Awards for best original screenplay:

```
==============================================================


                     ARCHIBALD
                      (mad)
         What does this mean to you're script?
         Every time a reader reads you're script,
         their bounced out of it because its
         you're mistakes that our doing that
         affect. Your warned! Again and again!
                      (tired)
         But whose going to care?
         Two many scripts too read!
         Readers will rather lie down and throw
         you're script then read it.
         Pleese, lets make a pack and get are
         format perfect…


==============================================================
```

*However, despite the need for good grammar, writers have managed to carve out one exception from the lexicon for themselves: **Sentence Fragments.***

These bits of sentences, sometimes without even a verb, are tolerated in specific screenwriting instances despite being grammatically problematic for the creative writing purists; some screenwriters actually relish in using them with profusion because they definitely help to create the mood of the story. They also help the reader feel the rhythm and the pace of the events as narrated on screen: by simply making the reader feel how long the depicted actions actually stay on screen.

But punctuation, including periods, commas, semi-colons or colons is still strictly required in your script. It is imperative that you understand the exact meaning of each one of these.

*Please note: a **semi-colon** is not the same as a **colon**. A **period** does not really convey the same feeling as a **comma**. And an **ellipsis** definitely cannot become your crutch through a lengthy dialogue or description as you try to infuse it with some sort of extra meaning that nobody gets anyway.*

Look at it this way: readers don't have the slightest inclination to read any text filled with grammatical blunders. So don't ever send your screenplays to producers or studios without first using your spell-check and several proofreaders.

Now, at the risk of repeating what many teachers have probably repeated in countless classes, your computer spell-check system is not going to suffice: the context of a sentence matters more! That context is what will actually guide you to write a noun or a pronoun in a different way than what your computer tells you! So, think before blindly following your spell-check!

And as I am putting these words on the page, I am keenly aware of the many times I had to override what my computer was telling me to correct or change, with a truly exasperated reaction: "Oh come on! What the hell do you know and who is the idiot who programmed you!" And that's probably the most polite expletive I uttered…

Here is Richard again, rushing into his repugnant bedroom. Notice the many sentence fragments without verbs, pronouns or articles.

```
================================================================

INT. RICHARD'S BEDROOM — LATE NIGHT

A tiny, windowless, filthy prison-like enclosure.

On a disgusting garbage-laden sink, rats and cockroaches
fight over scraps of pizza.

A messy bed and a rickety night table face the broken door
laden with a multitude of corroded chains and locks.

Suddenly, the sound of a LOCK! Hurried and insistent…

The door comes to life as Richard PUSHES his way in.

He quickly SLAMS it, hastily LOCKING all the chains in a
cacophony of metallic SHRIEKS.

================================================================
```

43/ Script Turnoffs

*If you have successfully navigated all the preceding
warnings, there still might be some other turnoffs lurking
on your way, and they could invite the readers to disregard
your opus, despite a clearly professional presentation.*

*But here is my dilemma: in trying to introduce what
the very jaded and tired producers and executives consider
as serious turnoffs, I realize that I have to bring forward
issues that I have never addressed in this textbook. Such
as **conflict, structure, plots, story hooks, climax, plot
points,** and so much more.*

*However, this being a basic screenwriting textbook, I
feel comfortable addressing these issues without really
entering into the specifics. After all, this textbook
should complement what is discussed in class and vice
versa! I am positive that by now, any screenwriting student
who is taking any screenwriting classes while using this
book is familiar with these concepts.*

So, here are your other possible turnoffs, in no particular order:

- *Your story lacks a hook*
- *Your setting and locations are familiar or overused*
- *There is no variety of spaces*
- *Your scenes lack purpose*
- *You lack a fundamental conflict*
- *The story does not engage the reader*
- *Your structure is weak or non-existent*
- *Your characters are poorly developed or clichéd*
- *Your dialogue is non-distinctive, stilted, stiff, wooden, predictable, on-the-nose and/or lacks subtext*
- *Your writing is confusing, unclear, lacks conciseness*
- *Your ending is predictable*
- *You lack a climax*
- *Your plot points are all over the place*
- *Etc.*

What to do in these cases? Rewrite! Rewrite! Rewrite!

44/ The Rewrite

I know: you've already spent sleepless nights, you've just emerged from that grueling writing process and you've truly given it your best. This is it… this is your absolute best script ever! It seems that there is no way you can ever do better.

Guess what? You can! And actually, you will… That's what rewrites are all about.

William Goldman, *a master of rewrites (since he is paid tons of money to rewrite other people's bad writing,) reminds us of a basic axiom:* ***"A good writer is not somebody who knows how to write — but how to rewrite."*** *And my late teacher,* ***Frank Daniel,*** *used to insist that* ***"Screenwriting is nothing else but rewriting! That's all it is."***

Leslie Dixon, Outrageous Fortune's *writer looks at the phenomenon with a huge dose of pragmatism:* ***"Rewriting is***

the name of the game. Anybody who writes a first draft and thinks it's brilliant and perfect is never going to make it in this business."

Same with **Emma Thompson,** *who must have shed a lot of tears through her rewritings:* **"With Sense and Sensibility, when it came to having to do a major rewrite, and I've done several, there were tears, actual tears."**

Sobering words that put the rewriting process for any potential screenwriter in glaring perspective!

Rewrite is truly the time when your script definitely comes to life. If you are the kind that is impressed with numbers, let me put it this way to you: researching, developing and writing the script amounts to about fifty percent of your work. The other fifty percent is exclusively devoted to the countless successive drafts you will deliver during the rewrites!

With that in mind, and guided by the wise and sobering words of **Ernest Hemingway: "The first draft of anything is shit,"** how does one go about rewrite?

First, you cannot start a script rewrite the day after you put your FADE OUT on the page. You definitely need some distance, a few days if not weeks away from your script. You've been so close to your characters and their story that your judgment is let's say… clouded and your ability to objectively analyze your work is impaired at the moment. Get some distance and you will be able to rationally apply some **critical thinking** to a candid review of your script.

Second, your rough draft was definitely written with all the passion that consumed you, as fast as your fingers were able to type, but without necessarily applying all your knowledge of the craft. If while writing you spent all your time applying what you learned about the craft, you wouldn't have been able to even finish that rough draft! That's why in screenwriting we need two distinct periods of writing: the **creative writing** and the **analytic writing.** The first one leads to a rough draft, the second one leads to a series of successive rewrites that will hopefully turn your script into a real work of art!

To put it in simple terms, you can't really learn without mistakes! Despite all the preparation and all the preparatory works that is supposed to get you to know your story and your characters perfectly, you will still make mistakes when you finally start writing: leaving characters unresolved, developing a scene without conflict, entering a scene too early, missing the right climax, relying too much on dialogue, etc. That's what rewrites are needed for: applying your knowledge of the craft to properly correct the mistakes and reach much better drafts as you advance.

Third, how to apply that knowledge of the craft? By asking yourself a series of questions and answering them as objectively as possible. Again, here is another axiom for you: **Screenwriting is the art of asking the right questions and answering them!** Later on, in the following chapters, you will find the questions you need to answer, in order to address all the problematic issues that can arise in a breakdown or in a rough draft. And voila!

Easy to say, not easy to do and not easy to repeat until you hate yourself and your script… That's what classes are supposed to help you learn and master! That is how to do it without hating yourself!

But having a mentor, someone to help you with this process, not necessarily a friend, but someone who actually could tell you objectively what's wrong with your work, is definitely a plus. And that's why teachers and script doctors are so essential through the process, albeit you will find even professional screenwriters who frown upon that kind of collaboration.

Finally, a question that keeps coming with every single student: how many drafts are needed? The answer is actually simple: **Nobody knows!** Once you get all the notes and the comments and the answers to all the questions I referred to above, don't even think that you would be able to address all of them in your second draft… The reality is, you can tackle only some of them in a second draft, others in the third, and other ones in the fifth or tenth draft! The goal is simply to improve your script from draft to draft as you rewrite.

So much so that the real professionals who spend their days rewriting ad nauseam, came to live stoically by a slightly altered axiom taken from **Ernest Hemingway** and applied to screenwriting: **"anything before draft ten is shit!"** As discouraging as it might sound, they keep forging ahead, knowing full well that maybe draft seventeen will be the right one, the Academy Award Winner!

But since each draft should be devoted to resolving and improving only one particular aspect of your script, here are the minimal successive stages you most likely will have to go through:

- **Rewrite One:** *Motivating all the actions in the story and understanding all its aspects.*

- **Rewrite Two:** *Review of the structure and the plot with an emphasis on all key turning points of your story such as break of the routine, plot point one, midpoint or climax, etc.*

- **Rewrite Three:** *This draft is entirely devoted to the characters, their motivations and whether they really are needed or resolved.*

- **Rewrite Four:** *The dialogue and how expressive, focused, necessary and effective it is. Hard task, as no writer likes to lose his/her crafty words of wisdom… The goal is to cut the dialogue as much as possible, and to leave only the lines that are dramatically focused.*

- **Rewrite Five:** *this draft is devoted to review the writing itself, the style, the pacing, the sense of rhythm, the emotion generated by your words, etc.*

- **Rewrite Six:** *Also known as the **Polished Draft** or **Polish**, the one where you take in the entire script word by word. Is this the best way to describe this action, is this the best word to convey the mood or is this my best line to express a mood and many more questions…*

Hopefully you will get more insight and more mastery of your story and your script as you go, but you will definitely get more input, more notes and more comments for each successive draft from others, whether producers, agents or mentors. By now, you might come to the point where the script is "ready."

But sometimes, despite all the rules you religiously followed, draft seven or eight still leaves you unhappy… Something drastic is then needed, maybe an entire review of the story or its structure. It's then time to go to Rewrite One again, followed by Two and Three, etc. By now they are Rewrites Nine and Ten and Eleven, etc.

Now you understand the axiom indicated above about anything before the tenth draft being shit…

45/ Length

*One page of a screenplay using this layout will give you **50** to **60** seconds of screen time. So, **110** to **120 pages** for an ideal screenplay, usually means the movie will run between **90** to **110 minutes**.*

*Yes, as we all know, movies tend to be longer these days, much longer than they probably should be. Action movies usually run anywhere between **110** and **119** pages, unless you happen to be an established screenwriter or director with a long track record of blockbuster successes. Then a **140** or **150** page script would probably not deter a studio from betting their money on you.*

*On the other hand, comedies and horror scripts are known to be generally on the shorter side: Between **90** and **100** pages. Why? Because comedies and horror flicks usually require a faster rhythm.*

*But if you happen to not yet be part of the exclusive pantheon of successful screenwriters, the conventional wisdom is to keep your script under the deadly **120** pages! Remember, psychologically, a reader is more inclined to read **119** than **120 pages**. Go figure!*

It's just like shoppers who are willing to pay $9.99, but not $10.01.

*Which means, you should never let your script reach **121** or **122** pages. For a reader, that's a sure reason to avoid reading it: How dare you not cut that one or two pages Mr. or Mrs. Screenwriter? You really must either be a lazy writer or you have a huge ego to think that your words are pure wisdom and could never be cut. Why then would they spend any time with you?*

*So, shoot for **119** pages, maximum!*

46/ *Your Title Page*

Title pages, like most elements of the screenwriting process, come as simple and ascetic as possible.

*About two-thirds of the way up the title page, place your title and center it. **DO NOT** ever put it at the very top of your page!*

*First, it should be **capitalized**, but **NEVER IN BOLD**!*

*Then, it could be either **underlined** or put **in quotes** or **both**. You choose.*

Here is what I have in mind:

THE STUDENT WITH A GOLDEN CAMERA

Or

"THE STUDENT WITH A GOLDEN CAMERA"

Or

"THE STUDENT WITH A GOLDEN CAMERA"

Underneath, after a double-space, here what you might unfortunately find in parentheses:

(First Draft)
(Third Draft)
(Penultimate Draft)
(Final Draft)
(Ultimate Draft)
(Polish)

*Well… Unequivocally, **AVOID ANY OF THAT**!*

*Like it or not, in Hollywood a script submitted to a studio is by definition always considered to be a **first draft**, even if you have gone through 95 drafts on your own. It could become second, third or whatever draft only once they acquire it and ask you, or someone else to rewrite it. So informing them that this is your ninth draft is futile, laughable and definitely unprofessional!*

However, you might want to indicate the kind of work you are submitting, still in parentheses and under the title, particularly if that work is not yet a script or not intended to become a script.

Here are some possible cases:

(Breakdown)
(Treatment)
(Synopsis)
(Outline)
(Proposal)
(Step Outline)
(Pitch)

After your title and any indication of the above, if needed, and after a double-space, put simply:

By

Or the fancier:

Written By

Then add your name below:

Written By

Joe Unknown

Here is how it could look:

```
================================================================

                THE STUDENT WITH A GOLDEN CAMERA

                         (Treatment)

                             By

                         Joe Unknown

================================================================
```

Or if it happens to be your final draft:

```
================================================================

               "THE STUDENT WITH A GOLDEN CAMERA"

                         Written By

                         Joe Unknown

================================================================
```

*But **DO NOT EVER:***

> *Capitalize,*
> *Underline,*
> *Bold,*
> *Or put any quotes beyond the title!*

And ***NEVER EVER*** *put your company's name as the writer!*
Scripts are generally written hopefully by living and
breathing individuals… You will be able to indicate your
flashy company's name later.

After your name, finally enter your full contact
information, such as:

```
             Company Name,
               Address,
                Phone,
             Cell Phone,
                 Fax,
                Email,
               Website,
                 Etc.
```

You would be amazed how many screenwriters forget that
kind of information in their haste to deliver the script to
whomever… Just imagine that I am blown away by your opus:
where exactly do I send that seven-figure check?

All this data should be written in the lower right-
hand corner of the page. ***DO NOT*** *ever write anything on the*
left-hand corner, as it might get lost through the binding
process or when holes are punched to put the famous brads
on your script.

But please ***DO NOT:***

Include any illustration.
Put any inscription in any fancy type fonts.
Use any large point size.
Add any graphics or drawing of any kind.
Include any type of attractive slogan.
Add any smart logline under the title.
Include some fancy colors on the page.
Or autograph your opus in a moment of folly and
grandeur…
Believe it or not, I've seen a lot of that!

Here is an example of a title page that will probably
NOT *get the reader to send you a check:*

```
========================================================

            THE STUDENT WITH A GOLDEN CAMERA

          (A haunting Tale of Ghostly Terror…)

                      Written By

                   Richard Hillbilly

                      ☺☺☺☺☺

========================================================
```

Also, **DO NOT** ever date your screenplay! Who the heck wants to read your last year's crop?

Finally, **DO NOT** include your WGA registration number or your Copyright Notice. That would simply show how amateurish you are!

Remember: Legally, your script is automatically protected the moment you write the words FADE OUT.

I would even **AVOID** adding the traditional warning that most writers like to include on the title page:

© Joe Unknown. Year. All Rights Reserved!

Unless you are planning to send your script overseas, to a country where copyright rules are… shall we say… relaxed!

All the above elements taken into account, here is how the cover page of what could become your next award winning script should look:

"THE STUDENT WITH A GOLDEN CAMERA"

Written By

Richardy Still Unknown

&

Amy Almost Famous

CONTACT:

Still Unknown Fancy Films
555 Fame Avenue
Oscartown, USA 55455
Phone: (612) 987-6543
Fax: (612) 987-6542
Mobile: (612) 987-6541
Email: Unknown@boxoffice.com

47/ What About A Cover?

Let's be clear here: You are not required to have a cover for your script. Normally, your agent (and you should have one, but that is a discussion we will need to conduct in class) is the one who sends your script out. His/her agency will generally provide its own cover. So you don't really need to design a cover or even think about one beside the above-discussed title page.

But because I know you will try to protect your valuable product from whatever harm, here is what you should do if you ever think about a cover:

* Use **white** or **black** card stock.
* **AVOID** colors, plastic or transparent covers.
* Put one cover in front, and one in the back.
* Both covers, back and front should stay **blank!**

And,

DO NOT WRITE your title, your name or your company name on it!

DO NOT ILLUSTRATE it either!

Any of this will simply confirm your amateurism.

48/ Binding:

If you want anyone who is someone to read your script, follow these rules when binding it:

NEVER USE:

* Spiral binding!
* Screw-type metal fasteners!
* Legal-style top-binding!
* Staples!

*All you really need is a cheap **three-hole punch**, **two 1-1/4 inch** brass fasteners, such as the ubiquitous **ACCO #5 brads**.*

*But, **DO NOT EVER** put brads in the middle hole!*

Officially, this will make it easier for anyone to make copies of your script if need be.

Unofficially, three brads are simply bad luck by Hollywood standards. And Tinsel Town is known for its superstitions…

*Also, **DO NOT** use brads **shorter than 1-1/4 inch**! They are physically irritating and the pages of your script will have the propensity to fall apart when a reader opens them.*

*Conversely, **DO NOT** use brads **longer than 1-3/4 inch**!*

They are irritating and physically difficult to deal with, no matter what you do with them. And don't even think about cutting them: they tend to become a health hazard as the ends convert into sharp edges.

It has happened, and you don't want that to happen to you! In today's world of Facebook and Twitter and other social networks, you will be quickly banished from town before you even got in…

CHAPTER NINE

BUSINESS CONSIDERATIONS

"Writers are like hookers. We start out doing it for ourselves. Then for a few friends. Then we say: 'What the hell? I might as well be getting paid for it.'"

Molière
Author

49/ *Protecting Your Script*

Protecting one's script is literally the sacred cow of all beginning screenwriters! I have known many a student who refused to even share their script ideas with me for fear of someone (obviously me, or maybe other students!) stealing them… How am I supposed to help or mentor in such a case is still beyond my understanding.

Not that script protection is not an important issue! But it should not become your major concern, particularly when sometimes all you have so far is a bare bones idea for a screenplay.

Let me, once and for all, put to rest many beginners' concerns: **legally, ideas are not protected, period!** Ideas are available for anyone to take. The only way to legally protect your idea is to either shut up and never share it with anyone (what's the point, then?), or develop it and express it through a tangible medium of expression such as a screenplay, movie, novel, musical piece, painting or sculpture.

Once that idea is conveyed, say through a screenplay, that screenplay can then be protected with what is called a **copyright**, obtained from the Copyright Office at the US Library of Congress.

And you definitely need to protect your hard work, once finished!

I have no intention here to address the complexities of the copyright laws, but let me quickly introduce some basic rules that can help at this crucial moment of your writing life, that is after you have put that exhilarating and dreaded FADE OUT at the end of your script.

- To obtain a copyright for your script, log into the United States Copyright Office at the Library of Congress website: www.copyright.gov. Go then to **Registration**, choose the **PA form**, which stands for "**Performing Arts**", fill it out electronically, pay the fee (currently $35) and upload an electronic copy of your script when prompted to do so.

- Your application will take some time to be processed, understand months… But the good news is *your work is already protected as soon as your application is accepted. As a matter of fact, your script was already protected when you wrote FADE OUT… but let's not get into the legalese mumbo jumbo as I said earlier! Suffice to say that you have a copyright in your work as soon as you apply for it.*

- *Months later (currently four to six for E-forms and seven to ten months for paper forms), you will receive a **Certificate of Registration** with a **Registration Number,** and an **Effective Date of Registration.** That certificate in essence states that you are the copyright claimant in the indicated work. This represents the official protection of your script.*

- *Beside the official legal protection, there are several benefits that you are entitled to as an owner of the copyright in your script: the rights to **reproduce** and **distribute** copies of your script and the right to **prepare derivative works** based on your script. Other rights can come your way, such as the right to **perform** and **display** your work publicly, but those really pertain to performance, which means a finished movie, a performed musical piece, a dance recital or an art exhibition.*

- *The duration of a copyright protection takes several pages of the copyright law, with a whole slew of articles, sections, subsections, exemptions, extensions and other particular cases related mostly to the dates when the copyright laws were created or changed and whether or not a copyright protection was applied or re-applied for… But since we are talking about your current work, here is what the Library of Congress officially states: "**Copyright in a work created on or after January 1, 1978, subsists from its creation and, except as provided by the following subsections, endures for a term consisting of the life of the author and 70 years after the author's death.**" Looks like a prison sentence to me, but it does protect your hard work…*

- *I know the exhilaration that first time writers feel when they receive their first Certificate of Registration. And they will quickly print that copyright number in bold letters on their script's cover page. Believe me, that elation will not last* very long when you discover that you have to go through that process for every single script you write, and often for several drafts of that same script. Which brings the following word of advice: **DO NOT** seek a copyright for every single draft of your script, if no one is really going to read it! During the lengthy rewriting process, professional screenwriters usually apply for about three drafts: the first one they feel happy with (could be a second or third draft,) the last one they actually send to a producer or a studio for consideration (could be their twelfth one, numbered officially First Draft) and probably one in-between, maybe draft number nine or ten…

- Another word of caution: if your script is slated for use in the US, **DO NOT** write anything on your cover page. Professionals know full well that… professionals will do the… professional thing: that means, to protect their work with a copyright! However, if you plan on sending your script through the world, where copyright laws might be shall we say… less definitive, you might want to add the following note on the very bottom of your cover page preceded by the international copyright sign:

©Joe Still Unknown (2020) All Rights Reserved

This said, there are other forms of protection out there, at least according to the traditional urban myth. Here are two that still are used by screenwriters:

50/ The Poor Man's Copyright

You know that one: Put a copy of your script in an envelope, seal it properly, put it in another envelope, and mail it to yourself, registered. Once you receive it, do not open it, put the dated registration receipt with the envelope in your own vault, and voila, you've protected your work! If anyone steals your script in any way, you sue the culprit, whip the sealed and protected envelope to the *court and prove that you already had written the work on that particular date…*

There is one small problem with this scenario: you might have never written the property and you simply stole it and mailed it to yourself before the other person did…

You see the legal limitations of this process. Let's simply ignore this kind of unprofessional protection.

51/ What About the WGA?

It is understandable that writers would flock to the Writers Guild of America website for any of their writing concerns. After all, the WGA is their organization, it has been regulating the profession since its inception, and it has been fighting for the writers' rights during its entire existence. It also offers amazing benefits for its members, including credits disputes, health and retirement, which at some point become essential for many aging writers.

And among the many of its benefits, the WGA offers the possibility for writers to "protect" their prized scripts by depositing them in the WGA vault for a very minimal fee of currently Twenty dollars. Once you send your script and you pay the fee, your script receives a certificate with a WGA number and will be deposited for five years, renewable if you wish to do so.

I hear and read a lot about WGA numbers, I see many of them proudly displayed on the cover pages of many scripts, and I know writers who think they indeed have legally protected their scripts since they own a WGA number.

*Which is far from the truth. Again, let me debunk this myth once and for all: A WGA Registration Number **DOES NOT EQUAL A COPYRIGHT PROTECTION THROUGH THE LIBRARY OF CONGRESS!***

There are many reasons for that:

- *The WGA is just a depository for your work. All it does is put the unopened envelope in the vault and give it a number and a date.*

- *You cannot prevent the WGA from registering any work with an identical title and text as yours. Again, they do not open that envelope of yours!*

- *Your WGA registration lasts five years, a copyright lasts… remember that jail sentence: your entire life plus **SEVENTY** years after your death!*

- *You cannot sue for copyright infringement if you only registered your work with the WGA. No lawyer will take your case and believe me you don't have the money to pay any lawyer to do so… However, a protection through copyright will open the doors for a lawsuit with very little coming from out of your pocket.*

- *Yes it is true that a WGA registration carries some weight as it can prove to a court that you had the work at a certain date; but then again, we are back to the Poor Man's protection, and we know how that would go.*

- *Yes, the WGA can serve the purpose of depositing some of your preliminary works: synopsis, treatment, breakdown, maybe a rough draft… It is faster, simpler and can protect you temporarily. But once you hit the final draft, your best bet is really the Library of Congress and a duly certified copyright.*

52/ Screen Credits

As indicated above, **"By"** and **"Written By"** are really the pinnacle of the writing process and the nirvana for any screenwriter. You have the right to put these prestigious titles only if:

- *You are the unique original writer of the entire script and the story.*

- *Your entire work is absolutely original, based on no other material whatsoever.*

- *No other writer at any point was ever involved in the writing process, including the rewrites imposed by the studio and the shooting script.*

Which is, let's face it, a very rare case that happens to just the cream of the crop as they say.

In Hollywood, if you happen to be a beginner or not yet a writer with a successful track record, it is very likely that other writers will be commissioned by a studio to contribute or completely rewrite your script. That's why very often you see a lot of screen credits such as:

"Story By"

"Screen Story By"

or

"Screenplay By"

Then there is the director who has always been the writer's nemesis, according to the traditional urban myth… The director is usually the one person who has the absolute power to definitely rewrite your script to fit his/her own vision and filmic ambitions. And you can't do much about it, but grow that tough skin and hope the director will not butcher your opus, but rather seek your cooperation.

William Goldman, *the veteran writer of such hits as* ***Butch Cassidy and the Sundance Kid, All the President's Men*** *and* ***Misery,*** *who has seen it all in writing misery (the pun is intended!) finally gave up:* ***"It is the writer's screenplay, but the director's film - get used to it."***

Or maybe ***John Cleese,*** *the famous British actor, who, realizing the name of this game early on, preferred to muse philosophically on the state of the writing process:* ***"I am proud to say that twenty-three people contributed to the script for A Fish Called Wanda."***

By now, you understand that earning the coveted ***"By"*** *and* ***"Written By"*** *is very unlikely for the run of the mill screenwriters, and definitely not the beginners. These titles are generally established after a careful review of the entire writing process by the Writers Guild of America.*

Here is how it works according to the WGA rules:

*At the end of a production, the WGA is approached with what is known as a **Notice of Tentative Credits**. This is a list of writing credits drafted by the production company for approval by the WGA. The company also submits all the versions that the script went through, all the drafts, all the rewrites, all the revisions, all the "Pinks" as they came to be known, by all the writers who ever had any contribution to the given script, including the director through his/her Shooting or Technical script.*

*That process is known as **Arbitration**.*

*A **WGA Credit Arbitration Committee** usually meets, reads meticulously all the versions of a given script and tries to determine which writer had what kind of creative contribution to the final version of the movie.*

An extremely long, difficult and exhausting process! It sometimes takes months and requires sifting through as much as twenty or thirty drafts of the same script, to finally determine the few lucky writers who actually had a meaningful impact on the final film.

Those will get a writing credit and the Arbitration Committee will decide what kind of credit it will be.

Yes, Hollywood is insane in that sense and I am always amazed that movies are still being produced…

*On the other hand, a writer's reputation in Hollywood, the category he/she might be placed in, the subsequent salary they might earn, their standing in the industry, is built exclusively on screen credits. That's why it is so essential to earn the right credit. **Julian Friedman**, a Hollywood agent, understands that importance: "It is very important to protect your reputation. Your reputation is more than just the sum of what you write. It is how you inter-relate with other people in the industry - especially the key players: Producers, directors, your agent - and how good a team player you are."*

In a sense, you simply don't exist if you don't get a screen credit, you might as well be a… ghost. And some screenwriters are just that, despite the long list of scripts they contributed to.

Here is how **Neill D. Hicks,** who wrote **Dead Reckoning** and **Don't Talk to Strangers** sees it: *"There have been instances in which every line has been changed and still the committee can find no significant change in the screenplay as a whole. There have been instances in which a change in one portion of the script is so significant that the entire screenplay is affected by it, and credit is awarded even though on a numerical count of lines and pages the writer may not qualify."*

Which does not always bode well with screenwriters! Here is one who prefers to remain anonymous for obvious reasons: *"At least 50-60% of all screen credits are totally inaccurate. It can be very hard for a writer to get screen credit, even if they have written most of the movie. There are writers who have been nominated for "Best Screenplay" Oscars, and I know for a fact that most of the work was done by other writers. And yet the writer will get up there and thank the Academy like they wrote the whole thing."*

Mayo Simon, a television writer, on the other hand is very blunt: *"Some producers don't rest easy at night unless they have fucked at least one writer a day."*

Warren Adler, a novelist who wrote **The War of the Roses** and **Random Hearts,** doesn't really disagree: *"Most screenwriters I know are not happy people because they've been bludgeoned, cut apart. The writer is the lowest animal in Hollywood. If I needed the money and was desperate as a writer in this town, I think I would be unhappy 24 hours a day. Everyone gets accommodated but the writer."*

Producers and studios, on the other hand, have understandably a different take on the whole issue. Take for instance how **Steven Reuther,** the late President of **New Regency Productions** sees it: *"I resent when they resent the process. I think if writers want no input they should do readings at their own house. The writer isn't always right, and collaboration is by definition what moviemaking is."*

Lew Wasserman, Chairman of **MCA/Universal,** is even more blunt: *"No writer is ever going to get his hands on a percentage of my revenues."*

But here is one possible solution from **James Toback** who wrote such hits as **Bugsy** or **The Gambler:** *"If you're selling your script to a corporation, you have to assume there is a good chance that the story will be turned into* *something unrecognizable. The easiest way to maintain control is to direct the movie yourself. You ultimately have to pay to keep control, but if you care about your work, that's what you do."*

*Whatever is your personal take on this controversial issue, here are the possible screen credits the WGA's Arbitration Committee might award you, aside from the prestigious "**Written By**" and "**By**":*

* When you write a completely original script, based on no existing material, but someone (or two, or three) else, hired by the studio or the producer, writes the final draft, the Arbitration Committee will offer you at the minimum the following credit:

Story By

* In the above example, the writer (or writers) who was hired by the studio or the producer, and who actually wrote your script's final draft, based on your original script, will receive this screen credit:

Screenplay By

* When you write a screenplay very loosely based on a magazine or a newspaper article, a television report, some vague event or a remote retelling of some action, and you use only very broad strokes of the original incident or material, and another screenwriter is hired to draft the final version of your script, you will receive the following credit:

Screen Story By

* However, when you adapt your script from an existing material, whether a novel, a play or somebody's real life, you definitely need to indicate that information right away under your name:

```
================================================================

            "THE STUDENT WITH A GOLDEN CAMERA"

                          By

                     Joe Unknown

     Adapted from Jimmy Ringo's Novel of the same title

================================================================
```

Or it could also be:

```
================================================================


            THE STUDENT WITH A GOLDEN CAMERA

                     Written By

                     Joe Unknown

                      Based on

              Jimmy Ringo's Life Events


================================================================
```

53/ Collaboration

Scripts are sometimes written in collaboration, by a creative team (two or more) of talented people who share the burden, equally or not. Some do it because they find a certain compatibility between themselves, others simply because they are able to complement each other's talents, and others because they were told to do so by the studio…

*A good example of a writing team could be **Joel and Ethan Coen** (Fargo, The Big Lebowski,) **Scott Alexander and Larry Karaszewski** (The People vs. Larry Flint,) **Lowell Ganz and Babaloo Mandel** (City Slickers I and II, A League of Their Own, Forget Paris, Parenthood.)*

*In such a case **DO NOT** write:*

By

Joe Yet Unknown and Jimmy Still Obscure

*Hollywood prefers the more collaborative **ampersand**:*

By

Joe Yet Unknown & Jimmy Still Obscure

Or better:

By

Joe Not YetKnown

&

Jimmy Forever Obscure

*But you might still see the old "**and**" used between two names or more, mostly on movie credits, as a result of the involvement of the WGA's Arbitration Committee.*

According to the WGA, "and" indicates that all the named writers have actively participated in the successive drafts of the script without being actually a writing team, without necessarily collaborating in a creative way…

Here is how this strange collaboration looks in the credits:

By

Melissa Unhappy, Joe Not YetKnown, Mary Undiscovered,

And

Jimmy Forever Obscure

This is an elegant way to convey that someone, or a group of people, hired by a studio, reviewed, re-plotted, rewrote or restructured your script and added to it or retrieved from it some dramatic elements. They actually became your "unwanted" collaborators and they will share the credits with you whether you like it or not.

And again, there is the unavoidable involvement of the director, which could sometimes be very innovative, but also could in other cases become damaging and destructive, even with the most respectable directors. Here is, narrated by **Richard Walter,** the UCLA Screenwriting co-chair, a strange but real case of collaboration:

"The story is told of director Frank Capra, who was asked in an interview to explain precisely how he achieved that special quality known as "The Capra Touch." For page after page he rambled on about this technique and that one. At great length he discussed how he had lent "the touch" to this film and to that one. And in all of these pages nowhere was mentioned Robert Riskin, who had merely written the films.

The day after the interview appeared in the press, there arrived at Capra's office a script-sized envelope. Inside was a document very closely resembling a screenplay: A front cover, a back cover, and one hundred and ten pages. But the cover and pages were all blank. Clipped to the "script" was a note to Capra from Robert Riskin. It read: "Dear Frank, put the "Capra Touch" on this!"

Frustrated screenwriters like to use a less elegant term: **Butchered!** And truly, sometimes it does look like butchering! That's why you don't find many happy writers among those who finally get a deal with the studio, any studio, or any production company.

In summary, here is a sobering quote from **Warren Adler,** a writer who realized the bizarre screenwriter's status in Hollywood: **"The craft of writing a screenplay is more a collaborative craft than writing a book. The studio makes changes, the director, actors - everyone makes changes, which often result in the bastardization of the original concept. There isn't a single vision behind a film, and most screenwriters will tell you that if you want some control, write a novel."**

As I said, sobering...

But the old cynic in me cannot but remember the countless cases when the seemingly *"**butchered**"* screenwriter was pretty happy with the officially *"**butchered**"* result once the movie went on to become a huge critical or box-office success, or even both!

Just a thought…

CHAPTER TEN

YOUR SUPPLEMENTAL MATERIAL

*"Writers are all vain, selfish and lazy,
and at the very bottom of their motives,
there lies a mystery.
Writing is a horrible, exhausting experience,
like a long bout of some painful illness.
One would never undertake such a thing if one were not
driven on by some demon whom one can neither resist
nor understand."*

George Orwell
Why I Write
1947

54/ What Else Do You Need Beyond Your Script?

If you thought that you were done writing when you put FADE OUT at the end of your script, you are dreaming! Actually, you need a lot more beyond your script… For starters, at least the following documents:

A **Synopsis**

A **Log Line**

A **Treatment**

An **Outline**

A **Pitch**

A **Teaser Pitch**, also known as an **Elevator Pitch**

And finally a **Breakdown**!

Quite a lot of documents, especially when some of them can be pretty long!

Here is the lowdown:

55/ The Synopsis

A Synopsis is the brief summation of your proposed movie's content and a condensed version of your plot. It should never be longer than one page if you want anybody to read it… You might sometimes encounter what is known as a **Nutshell Synopsis**, which is a much shorter version of the synopsis, usually not longer than three to five sentences.

Here is what your synopsis should contain, and how it should look so that an agent, a producer or a studio or network executive reads it, gets excited, and decides to actually read your entire script:

- A synopsis helps you to introduce your story idea without having to even write a treatment. More later on treatments!

- As such, a synopsis is often considered a selling tool, and thus has to be written in the utmost powerful prose, in present tense, with dramatic *descriptions of the actions you choose to present.*

- *Because it has to be short, you should not try to present chronologically all the actions of your script. You know you cannot cram all the events into one page, so why try? Carefully choose the most important ones, choose your* **Turning Points**, *or your* **Plot Points** *as some call them, then develop your synopsis around them.*

- *Because it has to be short, a synopsis should never contain any dialogue or examples thereof. Again, you cannot afford that in one page.*

- *Because it has to be short, a synopsis should not contain any excessive descriptions of your major characters. As a matter of fact, you should limit the amount of characters presented to a minimum.*

- *Just as in a regular screenplay, all the characters' names presented in a synopsis should be capitalized the very first time they are introduced.*

- *A synopsis has to be presented in short paragraphs (usually four to five) precisely highlighting the acts of your story. For the professionals, it's a technical tool that could help to know how the story is structurally evolving, with the key plot points indicated at the end of each paragraph.*

- *A synopsis should present the title of your script, the location, the time period of your story, the settings, the genre, the conflict, your plot points, your protagonist and antagonist as well the very few major interacting characters.*

- *Depending on your style, either at the start, or by the end of your synopsis, your might want to include your log line. More later on log lines…*

Here is the tentative synopsis I drafted for **Stanley Kubrick**'s *masterpiece,* **Clockwork Orange**. *Note the exact one page, the four paragraphs that usually stand for the four acts, the clearly indicated plot points at the end of each paragraph, and the capitalization of the characters' names as they are introduced.*

CLOCKWORK ORANGE! This is London, in a very futuristic and scary time… ALEX, the leader of a violent youth gang, lives with his PARENTS in a government-sponsored housing project. He sleeps during the day and quietly ignores school. But at night, with his "DROOGS", he spends his time violently beating winos and innocent passers-by, looting, raping and exerting all forms of anti-social behavior. The SOCIAL WORKER in charge warns Alex one more time. Instead, with his gang they attack a WRITER and rape his WIFE. His droogs however are not too happy with Alex's arrogant leadership. To reassert his power, Alex viciously beats them up. But when they finish their next attack, they swiftly club him and leave him on the scene of what ends up being a murder, for which he is charged.

Sent to prison, Alex tries to gain favors by playing into various reform programs. Which does not get him close to release until he learns of a new program where criminals undergo a behavioral modification, supposed to cure them from any thoughts of crime. Alex volunteers and is selected for the program. He undergoes experiments a-la Pavlov that end up making him sensitive to any instances of violence or sex, causing him to fits of intense crying and violent vomiting. He also becomes very susceptible to Beethoven's music, which is actually his only redeeming quality.

The success of the program is so convincing that Alex is released after a public scientific demonstration. When he encounters the people he harmed earlier in life, he is literally unable to fight against their violent attacks. His former droogs who became policemen, the wino and the writer, soon get their swift revenge. The writer who, aware of Beethoven's effect, locks Alex in a room and blasts the music until he madly jumps out the window.

With a fractured skull, but keenly aware of what is going on around him, Alex recovers in a hospital. The MINISTER OF JUSTICE, who actually selected him for the experiment, pays him a suspicious visit. Scared of a possible fallout from his dubious policies and aware of the upcoming elections, he strikes a deal with Alex: the writer will be silenced, while Alex will receive a large settlement if he cooperates with the minister to save his political future. In a final vision of the corrupt societal upheaval, Alex ironically rejoices his conclusive "cure" through a climatic montage of sex and violence under the apocalyptic music of Beethoven, while the minister is obediently feeding him.

56/ The Log Line

Simply expressed, a Logline is usually a one or two line encapsulation of the whole concept and premise, and a dramatic presentation of your story aimed at highly enticing someone to read it.

A log line should express the following few elements:

- *The title.*

- *The main character. And by the way, you don't necessarily need to indicate their name or any other character name for that matter.*

- *The antagonist and the conflict.*

- *The hook and the uniqueness of your story.*

Once you verbally present these elements, if you made an impression, you will probably have the time to add the following:

- *The likely theme of your story.*

- *The genre of your story.*

- *And it would help if you could indicate how the story might develop without divulging its outcome.*

A lot to do in a very short time! A log line should really look like a catch phrase craftily constructed with several buzzwords aimed at creating that interest to know more about the story. Is it about a woman madly in love, on a mission to save the world and her love? Is it about a man trying to escape from someone he loves? Or is it about this father who uncovers tragic secrets when he retires?

Themes such as love, loneliness, obsession, murder, passion, greed or hatred will go a long way in helping you to craft a catchy and unique log line. Here are, with their permissions, a few examples drafted by some of my most talented students during their professional internships:

===

A SIXTEEN YEAR-OLD RUNAWAY lives at a motel with his little BROTHER, and keeps a violent secret from the people he works with at a convenience store. (Dain Ingebretson)

===

When a controlling FATHER suspects his DAUGHTER is gay, he takes part in an experimental and very unorthodox system for "correcting" homosexuality. (Thomas Kuhl)

===

A YOUNG WOMAN, pot-smoker and wannabe painter, after a full day of smoking weed, begins to live her whole life backward. (Katrina Filek)

===

A young OFFICE WORKER in Manhattan gets a second chance at love when he is set up unwillingly with a PROSTITUTE for a one-night stand. (Joshua Robertson)

===

The tables turn on a biotech ENGINEER when she creates a genetically superior breed of cow. (Sharlene James-Whited)

===

Strange things begin to happen in an isolated rural Southern town when a clairvoyant BOY wanders out of the woods and stumbles into the lives of the locals. (Gabriel Siert)

===

BILL's got his own country. Uncle Sam wants it back… (Sharlene James-Whited)

===

When your "CHARACTERS" come to get you, do you play god, or deny responsibility? (Diana Fitzwater)

===

Obviously, a short script also needs a log line. Here are a few short script log lines, drafted again by some of my students during their internships:

===

A would be REAL ESTATE MOGUL discovers that one man's trash can be truly another man's treasure. (Diana Fitzwater)

===

A GIRL copes with the loss of her beloved UNCLE by going for one last motorcycle ride despite the opposition of her family. (Andrew Santoro)

===

KEN's best FRIEND comes over for a visit, but little does he know that he's a ghost and Ken is the one who killed him. (Rachel Cheslak)

===

*And here are three examples of blockbuster loglines for **Avatar**, **Finding Nemo** and **Harry Potter & the Sorcerer's Stone**, used with permission from **Kathie Fong Yoneda**, former executive and author of **The Script Selling Game**.*

===

A PARAPLEGIC MARINE is dispatched to a foreign moon to infiltrate a colony of ALIENS who pose a threat to earth, only to question his mission when he realizes this peaceful new world poses no harm.

===

Timid and cautious, a FATHER clown fish sets forth on a danger-filled journey to rescue his son NEMO, who's been fish-napped and imprisoned in a DENTIST's aquarium thousands of miles away.

===

Despite the protests of his neglectful AUNT and UNCLE, a
YOUNG ORPHAN enters the *Hogwarts School of Witchcraft and
Wizardry* where he learns his destiny will be that of a
gifted wizard. But he also learns that he has to battle a
dark wizard with the help of his FRIENDS.

===

57/ The Treatment

A Treatment is a semi-dramatized, present tense
narrative prose, introducing your basic story structure and
highlighting in broad strokes your story's hook, plot,
primary characters, acts, settings, turning points,
essential dramatic scenes and your unique point of view on
the theme discussed. It should contain only sparse dialogue
indicated indirectly. Some in the profession erroneously
refer to the treatment as the **Outline**, or **Step Outline**.
There is however a difference between the two as we will
discover when we address this later.

Here are a few issues you need to contemplate when
writing your treatment:

- A treatment helps you mostly if you want to **sell**
  your story idea without yet writing the entire
  script. Which is a common practice in Hollywood,
  open for established writers with established track
  records. That is obviously not yet, you!

- A treatment also helps **diagnose** a story that has not
  been yet written in a script format. Along with the
  executive interested in your ideas, you could use
  the treatment to shape the structure, the characters
  and the plot until you get the story straight and
  then you start writing the actual script.

- A treatment is generally **5 to 30 pages** long for a
  feature-length movie, and **5 to 15 pages** for a
  television movie. However, in today's fast track
  Hollywood a treatment tends to be relatively brief.
  As executives get younger in age and shorter with
  time, it's not unheard of for them to ask for
  treatments only **2 to 5 pages** long.

- *A treatment has to **highlight** the important details and the most dramatic scenes without which the story becomes incomprehensible.*

- *A treatment **SHOULD NEVER** be a philosophical dissertation expressing your views on the world. It should simply let the story convey **your vision and your take** on the addressed issues.*

- *A treatment should clearly express **the unique concept** or **the hook** of your story as compared with other stories with the same theme. In Hollywood parlance, what's "the hook" of your story is an essential question you will be asked again and again.*

- *At the minimum, your treatment should reveal your **primary characters, your conflict, your acts, turning points, settings** and **point of view.***

- *As for **style,** definitely use short paragraphs in your treatment, quotation marks for dialogue, wide margins, standard typeface and leave a line of space between each paragraph without indentation.*

- *The **prose** needs to be dramatic, which means it must convey the conflict of the story directly through concrete and direct action. Avoid descriptions like "we see" or "the story starts with", or "our story describes" and the like.*

- *The **language** has to be highly visual, in present tense, simple, unpretentious, straightforward, never attracting the attention to itself or to your talent as a writer.*

- *In a treatment, **AVOID** all technical and camera indications, unless completely essential to the production and the vision of the entire movie. Say you intend to have the entire movie shot in one single long shot…*

- *Add a paragraph at the end of your treatment about **production intentions:** why such a story ought to be produced in today's market, what makes it become so successful and which category of viewers will it definitely attract.*

- *As for the value of the treatment itself during the development of the script, well… the jury is still out there.* **Lee Rosenberg,** *a Hollywood agent does not seem to like them at all:* "**A treatment is pointless, period. It is a bastard form, used many, many years ago in a system which is long gone. I can't sell a treatment; I wouldn't attempt to sell it. I can sell a book — I can even sell an outline of a book. But I can't sell a treatment of a screenplay because they are written differently.**"

- *However, story analyst* **Linda Stuart,** *clearly opposes this view:* "**The treatment is so important, in fact, that writing deals will often include a treatment stage, the executive working closely with the writer to fine-tune the story and characters in preparation for the screenplay.**"

- *Go figure! You could blame all this on Tinsel Town and its morasses and even superstitions. On the other hand, it's also understandable that smart people could disagree on processes… Who knows?*

- *But whenever in doubt, better be safe than sorry as they say! I strongly recommend spending some time to write an excellent treatment that someone like* **Linda Stuart** *could indeed require when you try to get your script acquired by a studio or a producer. And even if nobody ever asks for it and you are able to sell your script without it, it would at least have helped you during the process of developing your script! And that's not cheap change, as a treatment literally forces you to plot your story properly and put it on the page before writing the script.*

Obviously, it is impossible for me to include in this textbook an example of an entire treatment. I am not sure any reader would survive the experience…

Here is however, a short excerpt from a treatment for a script that has yet to be written:

==

When they prepare to land at the end of their very first trip, for unknown reasons, things turn ugly. Jimmy and his co-pilot frantically manage to maintain the jittery plane straight as they approach the airport, while trying to force the landing gear out.

Luckily, a young panicked OPERATOR in the control tower, despite the opposition of his colleagues, decides to call security while shouting to help Jimmy and his co-pilot with the dangerous landing.

The plane finally veers off into the grass as a multitude of emergency vehicles speed behind it. With no landing gear it lands hard on its belly, speeds for what seems an eternity. Then slowly slows down, and stops in the middle of the fields. A success for Jimmy as no one got harmed!

==

And here is an excerpt of a treatment of the famed **Alfred Hitchcock** *movie,* **North By Northwest:**

==

Thornhill meets with three BUSINESS ASSOCIATES at the Plaza Hotel Oak Bar. As he stands up to send an urgent telegram to his mom, LICHT and VALERIAN abduct him into a limousine waiting in front of the hotel.

Despite his attempts to escape and his many questions, they drive him into the TOWNSEND ESTATE, where ANNA locks him in the library.

Later, PHILIPP VANDAMM, the very polite boss of the gang, impersonating Townsend, and LEONARD, his second in command, ask him questions about Kaplan's itinerary and about some agreement, Thornhill protests. He is then forcefully held still while Leonard pours half a bottle of bourbon down his throat.

==

58/ The Outline

*An Outline, also known as a **Step Outline**, but also systematically confused by many professionals as **Breakdown**, is essentially an extended treatment that lists the individual scenes of an entire script in chronological order.*

However, there is a slight difference between an outline/step outline and a breakdown:

*An outline/step outline is literally a list of short paragraphs in **prose format** presenting chronologically each scene of the script, with maybe sometimes a hint of dialogue, direct or indirect.*

Here is an excerpt of an outline for the movie where Jimmy and his crew try to land their plane safely:

```
=================================================================

The plane lands abruptly, its wheels SCREECHING in a cloud
of burnt asphalt. It veers dangerously to the right, then
to the left as it tries to maintain course.

In the cockpit, Jimmy tries to maintain control of the
plane while his co-pilot frantically works the wheel.

                        JIMMY
                Slow down! Slow down!

In the control tower, a surprised young operator decides to
call security despite the opposition of his colleagues.

The plane taxies dangerously on its belly in the fields as
its landing gear suddenly breaks, moves around a bit, but
manages to stop without further damage and without anyone
getting harmed. A success for Jimmy and his crew on his
first flight.

=================================================================
```

*And here is an excerpt of an outline for the famed **Alfred Hitchcock** movie, **North By Northwest**:*

```
================================================================
```

Thornhill meets with three BUSINESS ASSOCIATES at the Plaza Hotel Oak Bar. As he stands up to send an urgent telegram to his mom, LICHT and VALERIAN, two well-dressed goons assume he is George Kaplan, the spy they are looking for, and swiftly abduct him into a limousine waiting in front of the hotel.

Unable to humorously get an answer to where they are taking him, Thornhill attempts to escape, but the limousine doors are locked.

When they reach the TOWNSEND ESTATE, Thornhill is admitted into the library by ANNA and locked in.

Later, PHILIPP VANDAMM, the very polite boss of the gang, impersonating Townsend, and LEONARD, his second in command, ask him how much he knows about their agreement and about Kaplan's itinerary. When Thornhill protests that this is all a big misunderstanding and that he knows nothing about any Kaplan, he is forcefully held still while Leonard pours half a bottle of bourbon down his throat.

```
================================================================
```

59/ The Breakdown

*The Breakdown is a more **technical presentation** of the same chronological list of actions in your script, with an appropriate slug-line for every scene and without any dialogue whatsoever. And just like in a regular script, you need to capitalize all the characters' names the very first time they appear in your script.*

Here is how the first example about Jimmy and his crew would look like in a breakdown form:

```
================================================================
```

EXT. AIRPORT — DAY
The plane lands abruptly, its wheels SCREECHING in a cloud
of burnt asphalt. It veers dangerously to the right, then
to the left as it tries to maintain course.

INT. COCKPIT — DAY
Jimmy and his co-pilot frantically try to maintain control
of the plane.

INT. CONTROL TOWER — DAY
A surprised and panicked OPERATOR looks on, then calls
security despite the opposition of his colleague.

EXT. RUNWAY — DAY
The plane taxies on the runway, fast and without clear
direction. Suddenly it veers off into the grass to the left
as its landing gear breaks. Emergency vehicles speed around
it, with blinking lights and SIRENS on.

INT. COCKPIT — DAY
Jimmy pulls desperately on the wheel, his face red and
sweaty, his eyes glued beyond the cockpit on a fast
approaching tower in the middle of the grass.

EXT. GRASS — DAY
The plane slows down, finally stops just a few feet before
hitting the small tower.

```
================================================================
```

And here is the breakdown for the same excerpt from
North By Northwest:

```
================================================================
```

INT. PLAZA HOTEL LOBBY — DAY
Thornhill walks to the bar.

INT. OAK BAR — DAY
Thornhill meets three BUSINESS ASSOCIATES. He stands up to
call a BUSBOY who was just looking for a Mr. Kaplan. The
Busboy directs him to the lobby from where he can send his

telegram. LICHT and VALERIAN, two well-dressed goons, think he is "Kaplan."

INT. LOBBY — DAY
As Thornhill approaches the desk, Valerian and Licht direct him outside the hotel at gunpoint.

EXT. PLAZA HOTEL — DAY
Valerian and Licht escort him to a waiting limousine.

INT. LIMOUSINE (MOVING) — DAY
Despite Thornhill's pointed questions, the two goons refuse to tell him where they are taking him. He tries to jump from the car, but the doors are locked.

EXT. TOWNSEND MANSION — DAY
The limousine drives into the posh TOWNSEND ESTATE.

INT. LIMOUSINE (MOVING) — DAY
Thornhill ironically reflects on the posh mansion.

EXT. TOWNSEND MANSION — DAY
ANNA, housekeeper and Valerian's wife, lets the group in.

INT. LIBRARY — EVENING
Anna locks Thornhill inside the Library.

INT. HALLWAY — EVENING
Licht finds LEONARD, they chat.

INT. LIBRARY — EVENING
Leonard closes the drapes, turns on the lights when PHILIPP VANDAMM, posing as Townsend, the owner of the mansion, asks Thornhill about an agreement and his itinerary as Kaplan. Thornhill protests, Vandamm exits. Valerian and Licht enter, restrain Thornhill while Leonard pours half a glass of bourbon into his throat.

==

As shown in the above examples, you do not necessarily have to follow the regular spacing of a regular screenplay. So, no need for a double space between your heading and the description of your actions! As a matter of fact, in search for less wasted space, some breakdowns will have the slugs directly followed by the descriptions.

Here is how it looks like with the above example from
North By Northwest:

==

INT. PLAZA HOTEL LOBBY — DAY. Thornhill walks to the Bar.

INT. OAK BAR — DAY. Thornhill meets three BUSINESS
ASSOCIATES. He stands up to send a telegram to his mother,
and hails a BUSBOY who was just looking for a Mr. Kaplan.
The Busboy directs him to the lobby from where he can send
his telegram. LICHT and VALERIAN, two well-dressed goons,
think he is "Kaplan."

INT. LOBBY — DAY. As Thornhill approaches the desk,
Valerian and Licht direct him outside the hotel at gunpoint
EXT. PLAZA HOTEL — DAY. Valerian and Licht escort him to a
waiting limousine.

EXT. PLAZA HOTEL — DAY. Valerian and Licht escort Thornhill
to a waiting limousine.

INT. LIMOUSINE (MOVING) — DAY. Despite Thornhill's pointed
questions, the two goons refuse to tell him where they are
taking him. He tries to jump from the car, but the doors
are locked.

EXT. TOWNSEND MANSION — DAY. The limousine drives into the
posh TOWNSEND ESTATE.

INT. LIMOUSINE (MOVING) — DAY. Thornhill ironically
reflects on the posh mansion.

EXT. TOWNSEND MANSION — DAY. ANNA, housekeeper and
Valerian's wife, lets the group in.

INT. LIBRARY — EVENING. Anna locks Thornhill in the
Library.

INT. HALLWAY — EVENING. Licht finds LEONARD and they chat.

INT. LIBRARY — EVENING. Leonard closes the drapes, turns on
the lights when PHILIPP VANDAMM, posing as Townsend, the
owner of the mansion, asks Thornhill about an agreement and
his itinerary as Kaplan. Thornhill protests, Vandamm exits.
Valerian and Licht enter, restrain Thornhill while Leonard
pours half a glass of bourbon into his throat.

==

60/ The Pitch

The Pitch is a short verbal presentation of your story, a brief and lively summation of your script in order to sell it to executives, producers, and other investors you will encounter when you plan on getting your script acquired.

When imagining a pitch, most people think of the very comparable synopsis. It's wrong, as they happen to be quite different, and we will discuss that down further.

However, the best comparison that comes to mind is a movie trailer: it's supposed to grab your attention by conveying the mood of the movie and providing just a pinch about the characters with a zest of information about the plot and a few grains of conflict, so that you are hooked and you immediately want to know more about the entire product. That's what a pitch should sound like!

Here are some basic elements you need to remember when it comes to crafting a great pitch:

- A pitch is **NOT** a synopsis. As opposed to a synopsis a pitch will be performed by you the screenwriter in front of one or more people interested in hearing about your story. So remember that fundamental difference: one is read, the other is performed!

- Like it or not, a pitch is a **sales meeting** where, not unlike a car salesman, you are trying to sell your script… which means your performance has to be dynamic, articulate, enthusiastic and passionate if you want the listener to buy your product. That's why rehearsing your pitch thoroughly is a must!

- A pitch **CANNOT** be the same for everyone you deem instrumental to getting your script acquired. A pitch is a personal performance tailored to a very special individual who could be sometimes a producer, an executive, an agent, a manager, an investor, or an actor, etc. All these people will not react to your pitch in the same way. Thus the need to adjust your performance accordingly, taking into account who your listener is, what kind of products they like, what movies they prefer to see and what they want to hear in a pitch.

- You **CANNOT** really pitch properly if you don't thoroughly know your story. Unless you happen to be an established screenwriter and you are pitching to a producer or a studio who knows you can deliver... In such a case, all you need is enthusiasm, passion and obviously a great idea.

- A pitch is **NOT** a grocery store list of all the actions and events of your script in chronological order; just like in a synopsis, you need to select the actions and the events that will best express the mood while conveying the story in a clear way. So, **AVOID** listing ad nauseam all your subplots and all the details of your story and characters.

- A pitch is **NOT** indefinite in time: the executive, or producer, will usually slate you for a maximum of half an hour, and that includes the presentations, breaking the ice, and maybe a discussion after you are done. 5 to 15 minutes is usually a good duration for a pitch. Don't exceed it, even if you happen to be enthusiastic and excited.

- Unless expressly invited to do so, **DO NOT** compare your script to neither one nor the combination of existing movies, particularly if they bombed at the box office. **"The Godfather meets Magnolia meets Alien and A Fish Called Wanda"** is not your best bet and doesn't make sense! Your script is by definition so unique and so original that it would really be difficult to compare it to any others... At least I hope that's what you think down deep!

- Final warning: there is nothing wrong with having notes in front of you while pitching. But **DO NOT** ever read a pitch to a listener! It's a double insult: **a pitch is a performance, not a reading session.** If you are simply reading from a paper, why don't you just give them that paper and they can read it on their own! What you need is to keep your attention as much as possible on your listener, to interact with them, engage them in your performance so that they are never able to lose attention or stray away from your story, no matter what extraneous distractions might happen.

Joshua Robertson, one of my graduates, presented the following feature project pitch to a visiting producer:

==

Think of your fondest memory. What if there was a special room where you could relive it? Imagine a man going into this room. It's cozy, full of books. There's a fireplace in the corner. He takes one of the books, sits, and reads. Suddenly, the room changes, turns into an amusement park. The man is much younger and walks with a beautiful woman. There's flashing lights, music, and a carousel behind them. They walk, start spinning slowly, then faster, and faster until everything is a blur.
Then, darkness! Back in the room, the man closes the book. This is how the Breadcrumb Bed and Breakfast works: books are used to spark your memory.

The Other Side of Yesterday is the story of SILVIE, a young and hopeful writer attempting to finish her book, who works currently as a maid for a spastic boss, EMMA. There are two rules in the B&B: to never disturb Emma's sickly son, COLIN, or not to go into the mysterious room of memories. Silvie follows these rules while trying to find an ending to her book.

One day, she befriends a regular named DIGGORY, who has been coming to the Breadcrumb for over thirty years, trying to recall a special memory of his wife. When he agrees to read Silvie's book, he finds that the memory he's looking for mysteriously connects with her book; Silvie agrees to help Diggory restore his memory, and in return he'll help finish her book.

As time passes Silvie meets with Colin, and the two form a relationship, unbeknownst to Emma. But one day, an ambulance shows up and Colin is rushed to the hospital. Left to tend to the bed and breakfast by herself, Silvie ends up going into the room of memories hoping to see her happiest memory of her parents. Instead, she experiences her worst memory: the death of her parents in a boating accident, which Silvie survived and still feels guilty for. Emma brings Colin back home and is furious to discover that Silvie went into the room; but Diggory is able to convince Emma to not fire her.

With each day however, it's becoming more difficult for Silvie to focus on writing, as she struggles to come to terms with her past. In the meantime, Colin's health worsens and he suddenly dies. Emma goes into a state of depression, blames Silvie for her son's death, and acting out of anger, she burns Silvie's book!

With all of her work destroyed and against Emma's will, Silvie locks herself in the room of memories trying to recreate her book. But her attempts yield nothing like the original.

When she comes out, Emma fires her on the spot.

Left with nothing, Emma closes the doors to the Bed and Breakfast forever, and locks herself in the room in hopes to recover her lost son's memory.

Later, Silvie and Diggory meet for the last time; he convinces her to let go of her book and to let herself in the room. But Silvie moves on. A couple days later, she starts writing again; only it's a different story based on her own life, the memory of her parents, and her time at the bed and breakfast. She's able to finish this book, and leaves it for Diggory as a goodbye present. It's the story that finally gives him back his most cherished memory.

===

Note particularly the length of the piece: about one and a half pages! That's actually the ideal length you want to shoot for. When performed, it will come to about seven to ten minutes, again an ideal pitch length. As discussed above, a pitch is not a synopsis and thus does not have to be one page long.

Note also the many paragraphs and the casual tone of the narration, which is meant to be verbally performed, as opposed to be read in the case of a synopsis.

61/ The Elevator Pitch

Or also known as **Teaser Pitch**. This is a really, really, very short and quick pitch presented in general at a most impromptu moment.

Say you meet an executive by chance in maybe… an elevator; and you have the unique opportunity to quickly tell him/her what you are working on. Chances are he/she is riding to one of the higher floors where executives usually officiate. So how much time do you have to entice them? Not much. Maybe twenty or thirty seconds… A minute or two at the most, if the elevator happens to be old and cranky or if it miraculously stops right in-between floors… But don't hope for that.

That's when you whip out your most passionate elevator pitch with the hope that they will invite you to tell them more about your script either right there and then, or perhaps they will ask you to come for a more formal pitch at a later date. At least that's what you should hope for.

Usually, an elevator pitch contains the title, the premise, the genre, and the scope of your script when it comes to production.

It might be wise to structure your elevator pitch in sentences:

- One sentence to introduce the title, the place and the time period.

- One sentence for the log line.

- One sentence to present the characters.

- One sentence to establish the conflict and convey the genre.

- A final sentence to suggest the ending of your script, however, cleverly leaving the listener wanting to know more.

- And finally, if there is time, maybe one sentence about the possible cast, the costs and the likely markets.

172

- *But remember: just like a regular pitch and even more so, your elevator pitch has to be thoroughly practiced and rehearsed so that it produces the desired effect.*

- *And voila! Just look for those stray executives, agents and producers, randomly walking in the streets of Tinsel Town, riding the elevators, lunching in the chic restaurants, or even relieving themselves in the men's or women's restrooms… Yep, that happened too, and I am happy to announce that a subsequent sale took place, I am told…*

*Here is a quick example of an elevator pitch penned by our own **Jeremy Bandow**, a graduate of our program who has become one of our instructors:*

```
================================================================

Rise of the Gurgitator is the story of a gullible yet
talented film STUDENT who's forced to team with a gorgeous
but demanding INVESTIGATIVE REPORTER in order to save a TV
production featuring an Asian-American BROTHER-SISTER team
of professional hot dog eaters.

As both pairs get pulled deeper and deeper into on one side
the production of the TV program, and on the other, the
sport of competitive eating, they find out just how much
"collaboration" it takes to both make a movie and build a
winning competitive eating team.

In the end, they learn that when the chips get you down,
it's best just to eat them.

This small budget PG 13 comedy will attract any viewer
between seven and seventy-seven who loves watching how the
underdog wins the girl and how the hot dog gets downed at
astronomical speeds by a professional Gurgitator!

================================================================
```

*And here are three more elevator pitches for **Avatar**, **The Mentalist** and **Harry Potter & The Sorcerer's Stone**, used* *again by permission from* **The Script Selling Game** *by* **Kathie Fong Yoneda.**

===

Assigned to infiltrate a potentially dangerous colony of ALIENS on a foreign moon, a PARAPLEGIC MARINE is torn between obeying his orders and protecting the spiritual tribe with whom he has bonded. His friendship with a female alien deepens into love, and in a final showdown, he risks all to help the aliens save their homeland.

===

An admittedly fraudulent PSYCHIC joins the California Investigative Bureau, using his keen observation skills and deep insight into human behavior to help the bureau solve crimes, but has a secret agenda of his own: his ultimate goal is to solve the murders of his late WIFE and DAUGHTER who were victims of a serial killer.

===

Despite the protests of his neglectful AUNT and UNCLE, young orphan HARRY POTTER is whisked away to *Hogwarts School of Witchcraft and Wizardry* on his eleventh birthday, where he learns his destiny is that of a gifted wizard. Harry discovers the true meaning of friendship, family and loyalty with the help of his friends RON, HERMIONE and fatherly PROFESSOR DUMBELDORE as he battles VOLDEMORT, a dark wizard who killed Harry's parents.

===

This is more or less all you need when facing the frightening period of your ordeal as a screenwriter: peddling your script and trying to get it acquired by a studio or a production company, with or without an agent, in order to get that coveted check, with whatever digits possible, so that you can hunker down in your dungeon and write the next masterpiece…

There are, however, a few more steps and a few more documents that need your attention and are an integral part of your professional life; and I cannot omit them.

62/ The Query Letter

When finally the time comes to approach an agent, a producer, a studio or a star, your best bet is to contact them with a query letter, unless you have been introduced personally and you can simply rely on a phone call you know they will return.

A query letter is nothing but a short pitch presenting you and your script (better to have more than one to propose, three being the ideal number) to the potential entity that will hopefully request to read your script.

__A WARNING__: when sending a query letter, do not ever send any script with it! If you do so, your script will be either recycled, or returned to you without even being opened. More about this later!

What should a query letter look like? What should you include in it? Who should be the addressee?

Here are some basic considerations when crafting your query:

- *It should be short, __NO MORE__ than one page, and single spaced with __NO__ typos or grammatical errors!*

- *__NO__ fancy letterhead, __NO__ smudges, and __NO__ handwriting! Just plain white paper, clean layout, and double-spaced between paragraphs.*

- *__DON'T__ be funny, or cute, or obnoxious in trying to attract attention!*

- *A query letter is __NOT__ a mass mailing sent to 700 agents or producers! It is strictly addressed to one individual, tailored to a specific person you have hopefully researched. So __DO NOT__ butcher their name, qualification or address!*

- A query letter usually **should contain** three to four clearly delineated paragraphs.

- In the **first paragraph** you introduce yourself: work, education, writing experience, contests and rewards, and definitely emphasize the mutual friend or acquaintance that referred you to this person.

- The **second paragraph** should present the script you would like your addressee to read. Use your log line in this part and make sure you indicate the genre of your script.

- The **third paragraph (if you have three!)** should be about how you can be contacted in case the person wishes to indeed read your script. If you happen not to live in LA, it could also indicate if you are able to travel to Tinsel Town as needed.

- The **fourth paragraph (if you have three or more)**, could introduce other log lines of other scripts you wrote and you would hope the agent could be interested in. In this case, the preceding paragraph becomes your fourth one…

- This order is obviously not set in stone. I have seen query letters that started with a log line presenting a strong hook and concept. If the person who referred you were any big name in the business, I would definitely start my letter with that name. And if you have already lined up a great director or a star to package your script, this is what I would emphasize before anything else. They might not need more than that to actually read your work!

- At the end, write something like **Sincerely** or **Respectfully,** or **Cordially,** sign your letter and print your name below.

- As to **potential recipients**, do your research thoroughly. You want to make sure that you are sending it to a company or an agency that actually accept unsolicited works. For whatever reasons, of which limiting the flow of solicitations is a big one, Tinsel Town is divided into two clear camps: companies that accept **unsolicited** material, which means they would conditionally read a material they *never asked you to send, and companies that would accept only **solicited** material, that is the one they expressly asked you to send over for review. There are available lists for both camps, but it's not unheard of, if you have the right referral, to approach a company that does not normally accept unsolicited works, and convince it to accept your script…*

- *In this age of the **Internet**, queries could be emailed as well. They should be adapted to even shorter formats in order to accommodate the very short attention span people have acquired with electronic communication. But I can attest to the fact that a written query letter is still more effective and more regarded when in the form of a plain traditional letter.*

- ***Social Media** is definitely not appropriate for query letters. Certainly not Facebook, not Twitter, nor any other outfit existing or yet to be discovered. Although I wish some query letters would not have been longer than 140 characters!*

Here is a basic query letter without recommendation:

```
===============================================================

Date


Mr./Ms./Mrs. Amazing Producer
Successful Production Company
7777 Celebrity Avenue
Beautiful Ville, CA, 77777


Dear Mr. Amazing:

I recently graduated from the North Central Esteemed
College Screenwriting Program, and since I have been
regularly writing screenplays and winning awards such as
The Poor Writers Award and the Never Produced Scripts
Award. My last script Never Again won The Primitive Writing
```

Award few months back and is currently finalist in *The Unheard Of Scripts Competition.*

In *Never Again,* JIMMY, a young grave digger is crushed when he discovers on his first day on the job that his first deceased burial is non other than the beautiful neighbor he had a crush on for some time! He is even more distressed when it turns out to be a murder, and he finds evidence that the culprit is still on the loose, looking for the only person who knows anything about the murder, Jimmy himself!

I would love to send the complete script for your review and possible acquisition. I've enclosed a stamped postcard along with a SASE for your reply; however, you may contact me by email at JoeUnknown@Neverheardof.com or also call me any time at 999-123-4567.

Thank you for your time and consideration.

Sincerely,

(Signature)

Name

===

If your letter is addressed to an agent and you are seeking representation, you might want to add another paragraph or two where you introduce more about your achievements and more about your individual works and scripts.

Here is that case, and with an emphasis on a mutual friend's reference:

==

Date

Mr./Ms./Mrs. Amazing Agent
Definitely Successful Agency
7777 Celebrity Avenue
Beautiful Ville, CA, 77777

Dear Mr. Amazing:

I understand that you usually don't consider works from unknown writers, but my mentor and good friend *Joe Celebrity* whom you represented so successfully over the past five years, recommended that I contact you as my profile matches the kind of writers you like to represent.

I recently graduated from the *North Central Esteemed College Screenwriting Program*, and I have since been regularly writing scripts and winning awards such as *The Poor Writers Award* and the *Never Produced Scripts Award*. My first script, *Never Again* won *The Primitive Writing Award* a few months back; and my last one, *A Gift From Hell* is currently finalist in *The Unheard Of Scripts Competition*.

In *Never Again*, JIMMY, a young grave digger is crushed when he discovers on his first day on the job that his first deceased burial is non other than the beautiful neighbor he had a crush on for some time! He is even more distressed when it turns out to be a murder, and he finds evidence that the culprit is still on the loose, looking for the only person who knows anything about the murder, Jimmy himself!

What if all you heard about your wedding night turned out to be sheer lies? *A Gift From Hell* tells the horrific story of DEVILA WITCH, a hopeful bride encounters when her wedding night turns inexorably into a bloodbath, literally from… hell!

I would love to send the complete scripts for your review and possible representation. I've enclosed a stamped postcard along with a SASE for your reply; however, you may contact me by email at JoeUnknown@Neverheardof.com or also call me any time at 999-123-4567.

Thank you for your time and consideration.

Sincerely,

(Signature)

Name

==

Once you finally are ready to send your query letter, try to time it so they receive it in the middle of the week, rather than on weekends or on Monday or Tuesday: usually they are busiest in those time periods!

The next step is to follow up with a phone call, making sure they've received the query. Usually they will simply let you know that they will get back to you.

Finally, the waiting game starts… The best thing you can do is to immerse yourself in another script and let that one navigate the Hollywood jungle for some time before you react.

One of a few outcomes might take place as a response to your query:

- ***It is rejected!*** *Usually they will put that rejection in the form of a polite sentence saying for instance* ***"we are right now developing a comparable script,"*** *or* ***"this is not the genre of scripts we usually like to consider"****… And that's obviously the worst outcome to your efforts. Don't get crushed, it will happen to you umpteen times, you just have to grow that "shit-proof" skin, as they say in Tinsel Town.*

- ***You do not ever get any answer!*** *This is not a very professional behavior, but it happens. A last phone call to the agency or production company might get you a final answer by phone, as negative as it might be; but the writing seems really on the wall: you are either hopelessly wrong when it comes to the* quality of your writing or your research, or they are actual jerks with whom you probably don't want to work anyways…

- *The letter is returned, unopened!* Usually a short and terse note with it would say in essence: **"Sorry, but we do not accept unsolicited material!"** Again, that was your mistake, as you should have researched what the company policy was in regards to accepting unsolicited materials.

- *They would probably read it if it is submitted by an agent or an attorney!* Agents and attorneys give them the assurance that they are dealing with professionals who know the game, and who would not sue them later on if they produce anything comparable to your work.

- *They would read your script if you sign a release form!* And usually they would include some legally crafted release form, also known as a **Waiver**, that basically strips you from just about every right, particularly the right to sue them if they subsequently produce any script with a comparable theme or idea. The fear producers have when they read an unsolicited script is they might implicitly enter into what is known as an **implied contract**… Which could become a basis for a lawsuit if they produce any work later on similar to yours without actually paying you.

- What to do in such a case: if you have no agent, you cannot pay an **Entertainment Attorney** to help you or send the script on your behalf, and you are really tired of trying to get your script sold after so many years, I would say sign it! You are going to sign a comparable one anyways if they want to acquire it. You might as well… get screwed now as opposed to later!

Here is a sample of the dreaded release form that so many screenwriters agonize over:

===

The Lucky Company
92000 Wilshire Blvd., Suite 12500
Beverly Hills, CA 90210
Tel: 310.123.4567
Fax: 310.123.4568

SCREENPLAY SUBMISSION AGREEMENT

ARTIST(S) NAME (S):

_____

PROJECT
NAME:_____

Attached to this Agreement, Artist is concurrently submitting to The Lucky Company ("TLC") a screenplay containing _____ pages, including title and all other elements thereof ("Screenplay" entitled _____

_____,

subject to the following terms and conditions:

1. Artist understands that because of TLC's position in the entertainment industry, TLC receives numerous unsolicited submissions of ideas, formats, stories, suggestions and the like; further, Artist understands that many such submissions are similar to ideas, format, stories, suggestions and the like developed by TLC or its employees or to those otherwise available to TLC. Artist further understands that TLC has adopted the policy with respect to unsolicited submissions of material, of refusing to accept, consider or review such material unless the person submitting such material has signed an agreement in form substantially similar to this.

    Artist specifically acknowledges that TLC would refuse to accept, consider or otherwise review the Screenplay in the absence of Artist's acceptance of each and all provisions of this Agreement. It is understood that no confidential relationship is established as a result of the submission of the Screenplay. Artist shall retain all rights to submit this or similar material to entities or persons other than TLC.

2. In consideration of Artist's execution of this Agreement and of the concurrent submissions, TLC agrees to review the material within a reasonable time from the above date.

3. Artist has retained at least one copy or duplicate of all materials submitted to TLC. TLC shall not be responsible, financially or otherwise, for any inadvertent loss of, or damage or destruction to said Screenplay. Artist understands that TLC's act of returning the Screenplay shall not terminate or affect any rights or obligations under this Agreement.

4. Artist agrees that TLC has no obligation to Artist except as set forth in this Agreement and that no other obligations exist or shall be deemed to exist. Artist further acknowledges that at this time TLC has no intent to compensate Artist in any way and Artist has no expectation of receiving any compensation.

   Artist understands and agrees that TLC's use of materials containing elements similar to or identical with protected literary property contained in Artist's material shall not obligate TLC to Artist in any manner, or in connection with TLC's failure to compensate Artist for TLC's use of the material, and that if any suit is so brought, TLC shall be entitled to equitable relief to enforce the provisions of this agreement.

5. If any material or any elements of material submitted by Artist is not new, unique, concrete or novel and/or is in the public domain and/or does not constitute protected literary property and/or is not original with Artists, then as between TRÇ and Artist, Artist agrees that TLC has the right to use such elements without any obligation to Artist whatsoever.

6. Artist hereby warrants and represents:

   a. that the Screenplay was created and is solely owned by artist and no other person, firm or corporation has any right, title or interest therein or thereto;

b. that Artist has the full right to submit the Screenplay to TLC upon all terms and conditions stated herein; and

c. that the description of the Screenplay contained within the Agreement is accurate and contains all the elements thereof.

Artist agrees to indemnify and defend TLC from any and all claims, loss or liability (including reasonable attorneys' fees) that may be asserted against TLC or incurred by TLC at any time in connection with the Screenplay or any use thereof, arising from any breach or alleged breach of these warranties.

7.   Either party to this Agreement may assign or license its rights hereunder, but such assignment or license shall not relieve such party of its obligations hereunder; it is agreed that this Agreement shall inure to the benefit of the parties hereto, their successors, assignees or licensees, and that any such successor, assignee or licensee shall be deemed a third party beneficiary under this Agreement.

8.   If more than one party signs this Agreement as the submitting party, then references to "Artist" throughout the Agreement shall apply to each such party, jointly and severally.

9.   Should any provision or part of any provision be voided or unenforceable, all other provisions or part thereof omitted shall remain in full force and effect. This Agreement shall at all times be construed so as to carry out the purposes stated herein.

10. This Agreement sets forth the complete understanding between Artist and TRC with respect to the subject matter hereof. Artist acknowledges that no representation or promise not expressly contained in this Agreement has been made to TRC or any of its agents, employees or representatives. The laws of the State of California applicable to contracts negotiated, executed and wholly performed within said State shall apply to this Agreement.

> I have read and understood all of the above terms and conditions and agree to all of the terms and conditions above.
>
>
> _____   _____
> "Artist (s)" signature   Date
>
> ===

Believe me, if this release form frightens you, I have seen many longer and more ominous… For anyone who wants to be awed, Google **George Lucas's Industrial Light and Magic** Portfolio/Demo submission form.

- Finally, the absolute nirvana for a screenwriter is when they receive a short letter stating in very simple terms: **Yes, please send us a copy of your screenplay for review!"** And guess what, there are no strings attached: no release form, no need for an agent, and no need for a $500/hour entertainment attorney… It's very rare, but it has happened a few times in history.

- In this unique case, type a short cover letter with the appropriate thanks and include it with your script and a SASE. Then follow up a few days later to make sure that they have indeed received your script.

63/ The Thank You Letter

Whatever the outcome of your query letter, whatever the result of your pitch or production meeting, it is essential that you show your good manners, help document the process, and maintain open lines of communication for the possible future, by sending a note to the company to thank them for whatever they did, or did not do, and to summarize what should happen next.

Here is a sample letter following a pitch meeting with an executive. Again, note the very simple three paragraphs:

===

Date

Mrs. Happy GOLUCKY
Vice-President of Development
Fortunate Productions
Providential Street
Hollywood, CA 98765

Dear Happy:

It was a pleasure meeting you last week. I appreciate the time you took to hear my ideas for *Happiness at Last* and *The Luck of the Draw.* Naturally I was disappointed to hear that you were already developing a series along the lines of *Happiness at Last,* but quite happy that you may be interested in developing *The Luck of the Draw.*

As I understand it, your next step will be to discuss this project with the President of *Fortunate Productions*, and I look forward to hearing his reaction.

By the way, I especially appreciate the way you and Jamie made me feel at ease — this was one of my first pitches and you really made it a pleasurable experience.

Cordially,

(Signature)

Lucky Forever

===

64/ Of Coverages And Notes

Let's suppose that you sent your script over to this company that wanted to read it. What happens next?

I hate to bring this up to you, but the agent or the producer you were corresponding with most likely will not read your work right away. He/she will hand it however to a **Professional Reader**. Don't get fooled by the adjective "professional…" **Readers**, (who actually prefer to be called **Story Analysts**,) occupy a basic entry-level position in a studio, an agency or a production company. They usually are at the best fresh graduates from prestigious screenwriting programs, and at the worst, they simply could be cherished nephews or nieces of one executive or another, finishing their college somewhere, and who are getting groomed for a better position after getting their feet wet.

Don't get me wrong! I like the position, when it is filled with qualified people… It's just that Hollywood usually relishes nepotism, which makes it difficult for screenwriters to stomach the fact that "an incompetent prick" (these are the words of an anonymous and dead screenwriter, not mine…) is the gatekeeper who will decide whether your script will be read by the executive or not.

For the most part however, readers are conscientious professionals, talented and ambitious screenwriters and very eager individuals who try to do justice to what they read in very stressful conditions. Try just once to read an entire script, analyze it and deliver a solid coverage to your boss in one night… Unless you put in an all-nighter, and that's darn difficult!

Once delivered a script, a reader must usually read it in the shortest possible record time and immediately deliver what is known as a **Coverage**. This is a one and a half to two page document, containing essentially a synopsis of the script and a brief artistic evaluation of the story, characters, structure, dialogue and format. At the end comes the very stern verdict of the reader: **PASS** or **CONSIDER!** Let me put it this way: It's rare for an executive to read anything with the ominous "Pass!" And the "consider" is as rare as… maybe warm sun in a Minnesota winter!

Another one of the many reasons why screenwriters are not happy campers!

But if you get the "consider" verdict, the agent or producer will at least read your first ten pages. From there on, it's up to your writing to keep him/her hooked. If it does, then the executive will finish reading the script. And if they like what they read, they will ask for what are known as **Development Notes,** from sometimes the same exact reader who wrote the coverage of your script.

Development notes are ideas, suggestions, propositions and solutions, as well as other… notes to make your script better. As opposed to a coverage, they could be drafted by a producer as well, or perhaps a director or an agent to improve the script, not to make a different one. They are usually very detailed and exhaustive (five to ten pages is common…) where the reader could find creative solutions for the real problems the script seems to suffer from.

Development notes are written in the following way: first, identify the problems clearly and specifically. Second, use simple bullet points to suggest solutions that could be either instructions or general ideas to help stimulate the writer's creativity and help him/her on the way to solving the problems.

As you draft your development notes, you need to address at least the following issues in a minimum of one or two paragraphs: characterization in general and each major character in particular, structure, story execution, plot, dialogue, etc. Once these fundamental issues are addressed, you can then add at your leisure any other category for your proposed notes. For instance, you could address the marketability, location, time of the story, rhythm and pace, catharsis, if any of these are an issue for the agent, producer, director or executive.

Coverages and development notes vary from company to company and from studio to studio. Even agencies ask for specific templates that fulfill their needs. However, no matter the changes, the principle remains the same.

Here is a coverage sample that production companies, studios and networks usually tailor according to their needs and requirements:

==

Awesome Productions

Coverage Sheet

Title: Title of Script   **Log #:** # on Side of Script

Author: Name   **Date Read:** indicate date

Form: Script, book…   **Read by:** Your Name

Length: Number of Pages   **Time Period:** Period of Story

Genre: Indicate   **Location:** Setting of the Story

Requested By: Exec's Name   **Purpose:** Production, adaptation…

Log line: Here you give one or two sentences that encapsulate the whole premise or concept of the story, as accurately as possible so one can read these sentences and have a good idea of what the script is about.

Overall Brief Comment: Here you give a sentence or two that encapsulate your overall reaction or critique of the script, so that the producer or agent can read just this top section and decide whether to read the rest of the coverage.

Assessment:

	Excellent	Good	Fair	Poor
Concept/Premise				
Story/Plot				
Structure				
Characters				
Dialogue				
Writing Ability				

Overall Recommendation: PASS   CONSIDER

Synopsis: Here you write a page or so, showing the broad strokes of the story. You must show all the story turns and plot twists, the key elements that develop the story, plot and characters. You must also give an accurate feel for the story's tone and pace.

Comments:

Concept/Premise: General comments on originality, is it overdone and familiar, is the concept good but not well executed, etc.

Story/Plot: Include comments on story development, the plot and how it plays out, the subplots, the logic of the story, timing, believability, etc.

Structure: Comment on whether and how well the script adheres to the basic elements of drama and screenwriting in its structure, like act breaks, plots points, break of the routine and climax.

Characters: Here we want to know if characters are distinct from each other; are they unique yet recognizable in their behavior? Are they archetypes of people we've all seen before? How true and/or illuminating about human behavior are they? Do they change through the course of the story or, in other words, do they have an arc?

Dialogue: Here you should address whether the dialogue is expository, flat, on-the-nose, contrived, etc. Or is it fresh, true, distinct and unique to each character, capable of getting the information across in a way that doesn't feel expository.

Format: Point out only non-conformity to professional requirements. This would not normally be on a coverage in L.A. for agents or producers.

==

And here is a succinct template for development notes:

```
================================================================
```

Awesome Productions

Screenplay Development Notes

Title: Title of Script

Author: Name

Date Submitted: Indicate

Date Read: When You Wrote Coverage

Type: Screenplay, novel, short story…

Genre: Indicate

Requested By: Exec's Name

Log line: Here you give one or two sentences that
encapsulate the whole premise or concept of the story, as
accurately as possible so one can read these sentences and
have a good idea of what the script is about.

```
----------------------------------------------------------------
```

Characterization in general
Characterization by character
Dialogue
Structure
Story and Plot
Tone
Marketability
Location
Rhythm and pace
Time
Story Execution
Catharsis
Etc.

```
================================================================
```

65/ My Final Take

Whatever your views, or the views of one particular producer or executive in the business, you still need these documents to start your long quest to getting your script acquired. Some will ask for a simple pitch and a synopsis, others will want to read a treatment, then your script if they are interested, and others will read only an outline or a breakdown, and a log line. So, just to be safe: have all of them at the ready! They will introduce you and your script to potential readers, whoever they might be.

It's easy for me to write "have them ready"… But in my experience, I found out that most screenwriters would rather write a new script than get through all of this documentation. For good reasons: screenwriters are not always good at craftily summarizing their stories into two sentences, one page, a few pages or in a short pitch that will last a few seconds or a few minutes. So, obviously, they hate these documents that seem so different from the very art of writing a real script…

Also, these are selling tools that feel extraneous and cumbersome, and they do not add a lot to the actual script after it is done. And who has the time to write them after overusing all your efforts to get the script right! You are tired, exhausted from months of writing and rewriting, you just want someone to give you a check and leave you be until you start the next script… What a drag!

Albeit real and common, these complaints are neither justified nor always true. Some of these documents have to be developed before the script is even written: they can actually help in the development process of your script. They can be very effective in shaping the story and the plot, they can give you a better idea of how your story progresses, but most importantly, they often offer you a chance to discuss with the producer the structure and the outcome of your story before writing any scenes that you might, after all, not need to include in the final script.

Like it or not, you need to spend some time crafting and polishing these essential documents, as studios and producers will definitely ask for some of them sooner rather than later. They are your real vending tools, your winning ticket, your trump, or your… kiss of death!

Which means, most of these documents have to be cleverly tailored to whomever your listener happens to be and what they are looking for. Once you have them on file on your computer, it's easy to review any of them in order to fit the particular profile of the person you are about to meet.

A warning though: **Never send any of those documents unless specifically asked to do so!**

The reason is simple: If they ask for a synopsis, send them one. If they ask for your script, send it, but without a synopsis or a treatment. You want them to read the whole work, not one or a few pages. If you send them a synopsis with your script, they will definitely read only that one page to make up their mind… Imagine that you were not in the mood and that very page happens to literally… suck! You see where I am going with this. As for a pitch, you never send one since you have to actually perform it in person!

And while developing your works, bear in mind the wise words of **Christopher McQuarrie** who penned such gems as **The Usual Suspects** and **The Underworld**: **"There are actually two struggles: The struggle to write something and the struggle to get it read. You have to attack both with single-minded persistence."**

You might also want to remember **Bob Bookman**, a literary agent at **CAA** who echoes these thoughts: **"A writer's concern shouldn't be getting your first script made as much as getting yourself known. If any script gets made it's a miracle, much less one from a first-time writer. I would be more concerned with getting people to know my writing; you will get jobs based on having written a good script, even if it's not filmable."**

Finally, **Leonard Kornberg**, a **Universal** development director, puts all this in perspective: **"When a script comes in, it is not the writing on the page that will get it purchased. It is the concept. The writing on the page will get the writer noticed and pull him out of the crowd. We will look for his next script and may throw assignments his way. But in terms of a sale, the impressiveness of the writing is not a primary concern."**

That's Tinsel Town, and you are officially warned!

CHAPTER ELEVEN

THE AWARD WINNING SCRIPT

"Writers are the most important people in the business, and we must never let them find that out."

Irving Thalberg
Producer

Taking into account all the previous principles and rules, here is an excerpt of that famous Oscar Script.

===

BLACK SCREEN:

It's RAINING cats and dogs!

Suddenly, the RATTLING of thunder EXPLODES, long and ominous. The rain doubles in intensity. A siren SCREAMS somewhere in the streets.

FADE IN:

EXT. DOWNTOWN MINNEAPOLIS — LATE AFTERNOON

A scary vista: The MINNEAPOLIS skyline under the most devastating thunderstorm ever recorded… A deluge!

SUPER: MINNEAPOLIS - SUMMER (1999)

                    NARRATOR (V.O.)
          Who could have imagined that a benign
          Midwestern storm could radically
          change the course of one's life…

Another lightning bolt lacerates the skies, followed by deafening THUNDER.

                                        FADE TO WHITE

FADE IN:

INT. DINING ROOM, ANDERSON'S HOUSE - NIGHT

The table is set with a miserable attempt at lovely china and crystal, cheap candles, pseudo-sophisticated silverware and almost wilted flowers in the center.

ELEVATOR MUSIC PLAYS from an antiquated entertainment center in the corner of the room.

ELEANOR, thirties, slender and amazingly beautiful despite the shabby kitchen outfit, adds some finishing touches.

Suddenly, the front door SLAMS. Eleanor stiffens, spins around just as RICHARD, late forties, with a thick salt and pepper moustache, enters.

He DROPS a shoddy suitcase at his feet, THROWS a COLUMBO-like wet coat over the back of the closest chair.

Surprised, he eyes the table for a minute.

                    RICHARD
          Pretty fancy. Looks like Better Homes
          and Gardens.
                    (casually kisses Eleanor)
          Where's Stacy?

                    ELEANOR
                    (impatient)
          I don't know… Upstairs. Well?

                    RICHARD
          Well what?

                    ELEANOR
          What happened in Phoenix?

Richard moves towards the entertainment center, STOPS the music, looks intently at Eleanor.

                    RICHARD
          It looks good…

                    ELEANOR
          Tell me about it!

                    RICHARD
                    (unsure)
          Jim is still in Phoenix checking on
          things. He said he'd call if they
          like--

Suddenly STACY, thirteen, tall blonde, unusually thin and sickly pale, strides in with a big smile. She sees Richard, jumps over to kiss him.

                    STACY
          Hi! Are we moving?

Richard tentatively smiles, but that's enough for Stacy.

>   STACY (CONT'D)
>   Great! I wish I already lived there.

And she runs back the way she came, all smiles…

Richard looks furtively at Eleanor as she brings the food from the kitchen. She seems nervous, tired…

He SIGHS, reluctantly sits on the closest chair, opens his mouth to say something. But nothing comes out.

INT. HOTEL ROOM — NIGHT (FLASHBACK)

Cold, cheap…

Richard THROWS his suitcase on the tiny bed, rushes to the air conditioner.

It comes to life as he PUSHES the ON button, for maybe two seconds. Then it SPUTTERS, COUGHS and wilts down in a whirl of SCREECHING sounds.

Richard SIGHS: This is not going to be a good night…

He OPENS the window, BREATHS IN, hoping for a breeze. Then violently CLOSES it. The glass BREAKS.

EXT. "THE GENTLEMEN" NIGHTCLUB — EVENING

A beat-up HONDA stops in front of the pseudo-posh establishment. Neon bulbs of nude women flash all over the façade. It's sleazy at best, despite the efforts.

EVA THE STRIPPER, face hidden, but all curves and boobs and satin, carrying a huge and expensive handbag, gets out.

She moves hesitantly towards the glass door. Her manicured hand, sparkling with jewelry turns the fancy handle.

INT. NIGHTCLUB - CONTINUOUS

Eva pushes open the door of the glitzy nightclub. Subdued pink and red lights everywhere, a curved hallway, then the main door to a large room filled with CUSTOMERS and NAKED WOMEN.

And in front, a small table with a crude white light.
Behind it, a BOUNCER who has seen it all stands, bored,
disenchanted, ready for a fight.

As Eva turns towards the light, her face suddenly glistens
with heavy make-up, sweat and fear: This is actually
Eleanor! Disguised as Eva The Stripper!

It takes her forever to reach the Bouncer using her best
attempt at a suggestive and sexy walk.

                    EVA THE STRIPPER/ELEANOR
               (mumbles)
          Hi. I am here to see Joel…

                    BOUNCER
          Name?

                    ELEANOR
          Eva… Eva Longoria…

                    BOUNCER
          Sure… And I am Brad Pitt!

Annoyed, he decisively grabs her with both hands, turns
her around, pushes her towards the door.

INT. BEDROOM — LATE NIGHT

A tiny, windowless, filthy prison-like enclosure.

On a disgusting garbage-laden sink, rats and cockroaches
fight over scraps of pizza.

A messy bed and a rickety night table face the broken
door laden with a multitude of corroded chains and locks.

Suddenly, the sound of a LOCK, hurried and insistent!
The door comes to life as someone PUSHES it, enters.

It's Richard! With a bloody face! Heavily sweating, a knife
in his hand, smeared with blood!

He quickly SLAMS the door, hastily LOCKS all the chains
with a cacophony of metallic SHRIEKS!

A Police siren WAILS somewhere in the streets, getting
closer and closer…

EXT. ANDERSON'S HOUSE — EARLY MORNING

The house must have been lovely and expensive at some
point, but not anymore. It's tired, faded and run-down at
best, in need of serious maintenance.

Eleanor DRIVES into the driveway, gets out of her beat-up
HONDA. Surprised to discover the space next to hers empty,
she quickly rushes to the front door, still carrying her
expensive handbag.

She fumbles for her keys when Stacy OPENS the door, a half-
eaten sandwich in her hand.

                    STACY
          I heard you drive in, I figured you
          couldn't find your key again and I--

                    ELEANOR
                 (impatient)
          Where is your father?

                    STACY
          I didn't see him. He must've left ea--

Eleanor quickly disappears into the house. Stacy is left
with her mouth agape, in mid-sentence.

EXT. MONTAGE — MORNING

     - Richard, sweaty and bloody runs like a madman into
an alley.
     - Two POLICEMEN, guns at the ready, jump from a
hastily parked car.
     - Eleanor backs up from her driveway SCREECHING her
tires.
     - One of the policemen FIRES at a disappearing Richard
as he leaves the alley.
     - Eleanor speeds up into a highway dangerously
ignoring incoming cars in a HONKING cacophony.
     - Another GUNSHOT hits Richard squarely in the back.
He runs another few steps like a ragdoll… Then FALLS
squarely on his face in a pool of blood.

                                        FADE TO BLACK

===

CHAPTER TWELVE

THE THIRTY-SIX FUNDAMENTAL DRAMATIC SITUATIONS

*"As far as I am concerned,
in the abstract there is only one plot,
and it goes like this:
A person or group or entity (an animal or an alien,
whatever) wants something.
Perhaps it's to survive a blizzard,
to get married, to dominate the world,
or to save a child trapped in a fire, whatever.
Another person or group or entity (nature, for example,
or a destructive inner self) throws up every barrier
imaginable to stop that goal from being achieved."*

David Morrell
Novelist
First Blood
Brotherhood of the Rose
Lessons From a Lifetime of Writing

*Screenplays appeal to large audiences simply because they tell stories that resonate and connect with viewers on very visceral levels. They touch us because they convey passions that are no different than the ones we feel in our own lives. Most stories revolve around issues and passions we have all experienced at some point: **love, hatred, hope, fear, awe, revenge, betrayal, victory, loss, misfortune, infidelity, sacrifice, mystery,** etc.*

Since humans started to tell stories thousands of years ago, not only do the same passions seem to be at play in all good stories, but the way they are developed, the way they are told, and even their internal structure seem to be very comparable. There seem to be repetitive templates, whatever the country and the time period.

***Georges Polti,** a twentieth century French dramatic theorist, after painstakingly analyzing more than two thousand dramatic works from all over the world and all written in different historical periods, discovered that essentially there are only **thirty six** original dramatic situations available to writers. In his seminal book, **The Writer,** he asserts that all stories of all genres must ultimately fall into one of these dramatic templates…*

*His amazing findings, sad to any creative person who yearns for originality, but funny and definitely endearing to his own students who never took his research seriously, are extremely helpful to any potential writer, and if nothing else, they certainly put stories and the art of creating them in a surprising and sobering perspective! Whoever said, **"we keep telling the same stories over and over,"** was certainly not far from the truth and Polti demonstrates that with panache!*

Read the following with an open mind. In today's cynical world, nothing in this list should be set in stone, or construed as an ironclad rule. Just behold the amazing repetition of the same old stories through time and space.

This list of basic dramatic situations could probably help you discover an inspiring story or two, build an exciting dramatic structure, and start that fascinating script. As you will see, many dramatic situations clearly duplicate, which explains the laconic presentation in later parts of the list. Dramatically, all that's happening is a change of situation. The dramatic structure is still comparable to what was presented earlier…

1/ The Plea
- *The prosecutor, the pursuer.*
- *The pursued, pleading for help, protection, shelter, forgiveness, etc.*
- *The force or power upon which the outcome rests and the force having the power to grant or deny the plea, usually wavering.*

2/ The Rescue
- *The unfortunate victim.*
- *The threat.*
- *The rescuer, the savior.*
  Different from #1 in that the rescuer does not waver or hesitate.

3/ The Revenge
- *The avenger.*
- *The guilty, the criminal or offender.*
- *The crime or offense.*

4/ The Revenge On a Close Relative
This is about revenge on a close relative for a crime committed to other close people, relatives or friends.

- *The memory of a wrong or a crime suffered by a relative, friend, lover…*
- *The avenger, related.*
- *The offender, also related.*

5/ The Pursued
- *The crime committed, or attributed.*
- *The expected punishment or result.*
- *The guilty or suspected thereof trying to avoid being punished.*

6/ The Sudden Misfortune
- *The victorious antagonist, appearing personally and bearing bad news, such as death, defeat, bankruptcy…*
- *The one affected by the bad news.*
- *The surprising turn of events.*

7/ The Victim
- *The cause of the misfortune.*
- *A weak or powerless individual unable to resist this cause.*
- *The newfound strength to solve the problem.*

8/ The Mutiny, Rebellion Or Conspiracy
- *The oppressor(s).*
- *The oppressed revolting or conspiring.*
- *The dire consequences and the surprising victory.*

9/The Daring Attempt
- *The one who attempts daringly.*
- *The object, off limits to him.*
- *The obstacles and how to overcome them.*

10/ The Kidnapping
- *The kidnapper.*
- *The kidnapped.*
- *The protector or pursuer.*

11/ The Puzzle, The Mystery
- *The victim, the crime.*
- *The investigation into the mystery.*
- *The surprising outcome.*

12/ The Striving
- *The drive to attain or achieve.*
- *The unexpected opposition.*
- *The resolution, one way or another.*

13/ The Hatred, The Resentment
- *The close people - relatives, friends or lovers — that one hates.*
- *The consistent efforts to destroy them, literally or figuratively…*
- *The realization, too early or too late.*

14/ The Competition
- *The fierce competition among close people, such as relatives, friends or lovers.*
- *The fight and the extent of it.*
- *The realization or destruction.*

15/ The Infidelity
- *Leading to murder.*

16/ The Insanity
- *Among remote or close relatives, friends, lovers or professionally connected.*

17/ _The Fatal Carelessness_
- _Leading to tragedy, sometimes unexpectedly, comedy._

18/ _The Incest_
- _And the dire consequences…_

19/ _The Accidental Killing_
- _Of a close one, relative, friend, lover…_

20/ _The Sacrifice for an Ideal_
- _Of self or other people/things for an ideal._

21/ _The Self-Sacrifice_
- _For close ones, relatives, friends, lovers._

22/ _The Extreme Sacrifice Of All_
- _For a passion._

23/ _The Sacrificing_
- _Of others for personal achievement or gain._

24/ _The Unequal Struggle_
- _And the surprising outcome._

25/ _The Perfidy_
- _And the extent of the unintended consequences._

26/ _The Infringement_
- _Of a lover's rule and its consequences._

27/ _The Discovery_
- _Of a past of shame in a loved or close one, i.e. Skeletons in the closet and how to deal with them._

28/ _The Impediments_
- _To love and the unlikely solutions._

29/ _The Love_
- _Of an enemy or how to love those we hate._

30/ _The Ambition, The Hunger For Power_
- _And the improbable consequences._

31/ _The Iconoclasm, The Heresy, The Attack On Religion_
- _And the outcome of such actions._

32/ *The Judicial Error*
- *The false conviction and the definitive justice or lack of thereof…*

33/ *The Unsubstantiated Jealousy, The Suspicion*
- *And where it could lead.*

34/ *The Bothering By Conscience*
- *And its outcome.*

35/ *The Losing And Finding Of Someone/Something Treasured*
- *And the surprising consequences.*

36/ *The Personal Loss Of A Close One*
- *And the impact and aftermath.*

CHAPTER THIRTEEN

THE CHARACTER'S FIVE P's

"I write about myself, my brother, my parents, my wife, my children, my friends, my coworkers, the people I meet all the time. I always try to write about them with some affection, but mostly with some honesty. And I have never once had anybody come up to me and say, "How dare you put me down that way." Never."

Neil Simon
The Odd Couple
The Out-of-Towners
The Goodbye Girl

How does one even start conceiving a new character?

Just like a painter or a sculptor who starts by drawing a rough sketch of their future painting or sculpture, a screenwriter begins most likely with a very rough sketch of that new character, based on observations, notes, ideas, characters we know or we have met by chance; and sometimes we simply make them up from scratch, infusing them with unusual qualities and traits that will turn them into exciting, believable and unique entities.

Here is how **Tom Schulman**, who penned **Honey, I Shrunk the Kids** and **Dead Poets Society**, sees this process: **"As much as possible I try to create characters who are amalgamations of people I know. I try to start with a face of someone I grew up with or met so I understand the basics of where that character is coming from. He'll probably end up in a completely fictional spot in the story, but you have to write what you know. You have to try to pin down your characters as much as possible to real people."**

The **Five P's** is a basic and useful exercise designed to help you draw that preliminary sketch so that you get to know your characters better. A rough draft as it were…

Jot a few lines for each P. of your character. Nothing fancy, expansive or exhaustive for the moment.

As a general rule, do not exceed one or two pages at most, using pertinent facts in a bullet form, not even in full-fledged sentences.

==========================

Physical Traits

General physical appearance, age, height, weight, clothing and manners…
Scars, birthmarks, physical signs or particularities such as a goatee, a beard or a moustache…
Does she limp a little, walk funny or eat obnoxiously?
How does he talk, laugh? Loud, timid, hysteric, warm, retiring…

Professional Attributes

Work, money…
Relationship with other co-workers or employees…
How does he/she feel about the boss? Or about
subordinates if he/she happens to be the boss?
Satisfaction from work or lack thereof, aspirations
and professional ambitions.

Personal Features

Family life: Single, widowed, married, divorced,
separated, from whom…
Children and relationship with them, good father/mom
or rather believes they make him/her older?
Is he/she happy with current status?
Solid marriage, good husband, wife, extramarital
affairs, faithful, religiously inclined or
hopelessly non-believer…
Friends: lonely, lots of superficial friendships or
just a few real ones, too many friends…

Public Habits

Your character alone, but in public…
What does he/she do when he/she is alone, in his/her
free time? What are his/her hobbies: Jogging,
watching TV, knitting, reading, stamp collection,
gardening, daydreaming, car repair, home
maintenance, writing, dancing, model building…

Private Peculiarities

Hidden actions or tendencies your character would
entertain when in total privacy. These are the dark
or sometimes laughable secrets she/he would never
want to share with anybody.
It might be as innocent as poetry writing, working
on his correct pronunciation, learning some craft or
dance training in secret, or trying to remove some
annoying physical deficiency.
But it could be, and it usually is, of a much darker
kind; such as addiction to porno flicks, rehearsing
for some violent armed action, writing anonymous
letters or even… strangling innocent old ladies on
Sundays.

CHAPTER FOURTEEN

CCR

THE CHARACTER CREATIVE RESEARCH

*"Creating dimensional characters comes down to
identifying with the character:
Knowing who that character is, what drives them
[What actors call the spine of the character],
what their background is, their speech pattern,
choice of words. You must get to know your character.
You really must have a clear grasp of
what that character wants in life,
what he's trying to get from the other characters,
how he'd behave in and react to any
situation you put him in.
But in many poorly written scripts,
you can put your thumb over the character's name
and not even know who is talking.
Something is lacking there, and it's because somebody is
writing with no sense who their character is."*

Frank Pierson
Screenwriter
*Presumed Innocent, Dog Day Afternoon
A Star is Born, Cool Hand Luke*

Characters are definitely the essential elements of your screenplay. Knowing them thoroughly is fundamental to your plot, your story and your script.

This exercise is meant to help you better build your characters, give them the necessary traits, the unique attributes and the quirky details that will make them so believable, that we viewers, will start to deal with them as if they were real persons of flesh and blood.

This set of questions, conveniently divided into ten blocks, is labeled **Character Creative Research** *or* **(CCR)***, simply because you are actually creating your character as you answer the questions. While developing and writing your script, a large amount of your talent will be devoted to asking the right questions and creatively answering them. Who, where, when, with whom, who is against them, what happens first, who is the victim, what is the conflict, what happens next, what happens after, and after, and after…*

You get the point!

A warning though: A character is much more than any list of attributes, as exhaustive as they might be. They are alive and well inside you. The problem is to get them out, on the page, in the story. This exercise technically helps you build them, but their significance transcends the page, the list of attributes you create, and ultimately the screen itself.

In simple terms, this means: Don't get hung up on exact answers and tortured emotional choices. You will most likely change some of it as you delve into your story. The beauty of characters is their ability to surprise you and to change within the story, because of the events they experience. **As Linda Stuart,** *story analyst asserts:* **"Character is plot and plot is character. They are linked."**

But more about this issue, obviously in class!

Final note before beginning your exercise: Some of the questions might not apply to your characters. That's all right! After all, if your character happens to be a nine year-old boy, I don't think a job, parenting or sex, are a particular issue for them. Well… Maybe not, hopefully not… At any rate, simply disregard the question and move on to the next one.

I/ Family

1/ Father
What does she think of her father?
What does she hate and like about him?
What influence did her father have on her?

2/ Mother
What does he think of his mother?
What does he hate and like about her?
What influence did she, in his opinion, have on him?

3/ Siblings
How many?
Does she like or despise any of them?
What does she like or despise about them?

4/ Discipline
What type of discipline was he subjected to at home?
Strict? Lenient? Negligent? Derelict? Etc.
Was he overprotected?
Did he feel rejection or affection as a child?

5/ Economics
What was the economic status of her family?
Were there any adverse situations, divorce, illness, alcoholism, drug problems?

6/ Religion
What was the religious atmosphere in his family?
How does he personally feel about religion today?

7/ Politics.
How involved was her family in political life?
What are her political beliefs today?
How involved is she now in politics?

II/ Education

8/ The School and its Impact
Did he like school? His teachers? His schoolmates?
What is his highest degree of education?
Does he see himself as smart? Intelligent? Uneducated?
How is his education and intelligence reflected in his speech pattern, vocabulary and pronunciation?

III/ Experience

9/ About Travel
Did she travel? Where? Why?
What did she find abroad? What does she remember?
What was she interested and involved in mostly?

10/ Impressive Events
What were the most deeply impressive political,
religious or social - national or international -
events that he experienced?

11/ Disillusionments
What were her deepest disillusionments in life, her
greatest regret, her greatest achievement?
How does she feel about them?

IV/ Friendships

12/ Friends
Who are his friends? Does he have many?
How deep or superficial are his friendships?
How fast does he enter into friendships?

13/ Groups
What social groups and activities does she attend?
What role does she like to play?
What role does she end up playing?

V/ Profession

14/ Job
What does he do for a living? Does he make good money?
How does he see his profession?
What does he like or dislike about it?
What kind of relationship does he have with other co-
workers or employees? How does he feel about the boss?
How satisfied in general is he with his work?
What are his professional ambitions?

VI/ Home

15/ Castle
What does her home look like?
How about furniture and decoration?

Is she happy with it?
Is she dreaming of a different home?

16/ Role
What role does he play at home?
What role would he like to play?
Does he like staying at home?
What does he do when he does stay at home?

VII/ Parenting

17/ Children
Does she have children? How does she feel about them?
How does she feel about her parental role?
And how do the children relate to her?
Is she trying to get pregnant?

VIII/ The Individual

18/ Facial Attributes
What about his hair? Does he have a beard? Whiskers?
Moustache? Does he use any make-up?
How does he relate to his own appearance?

19/ Expression
What is her prevailing facial expression?
Sour? Cheerful? Dominating? Bored?

20/ Voice and Diction
What is his voice like? How is his Pitch, his Volume?
How about the Tempo and rhythm of his speech?
Does he have any accent? Slang? Jargon? Regionalism?
Unique Pronunciation?

21/ Gestures
What are her gestures like? Vigorous? Controlled?
Weak? Compulsive?
Generally, is she energetic or sluggish?

22/ Clothes
How is he usually dressed? What style? What quality?
Does he care?
How comfortable is he in a formal dress?

23/ Manners
What are her manners like? Distinguished, polite, fashionable, pedestrian, common?
What is her type of hero?
Whom does she hate?

24/ Personal Feelings
How does he feel about his size, weight?
How about his posture, his walk?
If he could change one thing about himself, what would it be?
Does he want to project an image of a younger, older, wiser, funnier, more important… person?
Does he want to be visible or invisible?

25/ Hobbies
What are her hobbies and interests? When does she attend to them? How involved is she with them?

26/ Bad Habits
Does he drink? Smoke? Take drugs?
How does he deal with that? Does he lie? When?

27/ Sex
What is her attitude towards sex?
Who are her love mates? What is her type of "ideal" partner? What does she want from them? How does she relate to them? How does she make her choice?

28/ Health
What is his health like? What does he do for it?
Is he satisfied with it?

IX/ Psychological Profile

29/ Intelligence
Is she sharp, wise, clever, intelligent, stupid, dim-witted?

30/ Stress
How does he react to stressful situations? Defensively? Aggressively? Evasively?
How does he accept disasters and failures?

31/ Dealing With Errors
Does she always rationalize her errors? Does she feel self-righteous? Revengeful?

32/ Suffering
Does he like to suffer? Does he like to see other people suffer? Does he actively make other people suffer?

33/ Imagination
How is her imagination? Does she daydream a lot? Is she worried, cool, or calm most of the time? Or is she rather living in memories?

34/ Posture
How is he when he faces new things? Negative, suspicious, hostile, scared, enthusiastic?

35/ Ridicule
What does she like to ridicule? What does she find stupid, ironic or laughable?

36/ Sense of Humor
How is his sense of humor? What does he find funny? Is he aware of himself, his idiosyncrasies, and weak spots? Is he capable of self-irony, self-deprecation?

37/ Drive, Want
What are her fundamental ambitions, dreams, desires, wishes, cravings, fears? What does she want most and is aware of?

38/ Drive, Need
What does he need really badly, compulsively? Is he aware of that or is it strictly subconscious? How does it materialize in his daily life?

39/ Sacrifice
How badly does she want to get what she claims as her life objectives? What is she willing to do, to sacrifice in order to reach them? How does she pursue these objectives?

X/ How Do You Feel About Her?

40/ Your Final Thoughts
Do you like her? Do you hate her? Why do you need to write about her? Why should people be excited about her?

CHAPTER FIFTEEN

THE STORY IDEATION

YOUR FIFTEEN PRELIMINARY QUESTIONS

*"The fact that writing is a form of communication
necessitates being aware of structure,
because you're basically telling a story,
and stories have beginnings, middles and ends.
They have to grab you early, interest you in the middle,
and move you at the end.
That structure is at work whenever we tell
a story of any length, in any form.
So those things are only there to help you.
Where they hurt is when you get mechanical about them
and try to invent things which are external to the internal
logic of the story."*

Tom Schulman
Screenwriter
What About Bob?
Honey, I Shrunk the Kids
Dead Poets Society

How many times, when a sudden idea hits you with an amazing sense of urgency, do you find yourself tortured by the fundamental question: Is it any good? Does it have what it takes to become a good story? Could it lead to an exciting script? In short and to use the Hollywood jargon, "does it have legs?"

You know how tough it is to answer these kinds of questions. Yet, you need to know, now! You can't just work for six months on a project only to discover that the main idea was flawed from the very beginning. What kind of professional screenwriter are you?

How do professionals cope with such an uncomfortable situation? Well… There are no ironclad rules. Everybody conjures the muse differently!

*Here is how **Shane Black**, the famed screenwriter of **Lethal Weapon**, goes about it: "I have a shoebox for ideas, fragments, snatches of conversation I hear. I scrawl it down, throw the scraps in the box. Every time I start a new script I start picking through the pieces. Suddenly you get five pieces together and think: This is almost the first Act of a movie, if I flesh it out a bit."*

Not very… scientific, by all means!

*Here is what **Joe Esterhaz**, another famed millionaire who penned **Basic Instinct**, **Flashdance** and **Striptease**, advises: "I think there is a great danger for a writer to sit down and try to figure out what will be commercial, because you're going to wind up doing contortions. Just sit down and write what you believe in. The quality of the material will be better and you will feel like a writer […]. What you should be concerned about is writing the best story that you can as the muse moves you."*

Easy to say, but not necessarily very helpful…

*Here is what **Lew Hunter**, Professor Emeritus at UCLA, tells his students: "The word "tricks" is unfortunately pejorative. As are "gimmicks," "devices," "tools," "contrivance," "formulas," and "craft." I fiercely maintain there can be good tricks, gimmicks, devices, tools, contrivance, formulas, and craft. Here is one method of idea discovery that is a positive trick: The "What if…" trick."*

This could definitely help start the process, but how far can you go?

I personally approach the whole endeavor as a conscious working process that needs, just like any story, a beginning, middle, and an end. My "trick," "gimmick," "device," " tool," or "formula" is a very simple concept, known as **ideation**... *or conjuring the ideas as it were...*

Ideation is a cluster of fifteen pertinent questions that are meant to help you focus your attention, organize your scattered thoughts, analyze their potential for any kind of script, long or short, and reveal any elements or aspects that need further development or review.

Answer these questions as candidly, as simply and as frankly as you can.

If by any chance you can't answer some of them, don't force yourself, don't agonize over it! The exercise is actually working: It simply means you need to develop and expand that particular aspect of your story!

Now you know at least where to focus your efforts!

Here are your fifteen questions:

===============================

1/

Do you have a compelling protagonist with a powerful drive?

2/

Do you have a compelling antagonist with a powerful drive?

3/

Do you have a strong conflict? What is it?

4/

How about obstacles? Could you think of some?

5/

    Do you have any subplots? Any other characters that can make a more exciting story?

6/

    Do you have an attractive environment?

7/

    Why here, why now, why this historical period?

8/

    Could there be another time or place where this story would be more exciting?

9/

    What is the genre of your story?

10/

    What is your premise, your basis of argument? What do you want to convey through your story? What is your theme?

11/

    What makes you fit to best tell this story? Do you know anything about the subject matter?

12/

    Why should it interest me, why should I care?

13/

    How does your story end? Does your character reach his/her goals?

14/

    Are you really telling me what you intended in #10 with this particular ending?

15/

    Write a short one-paragraph synopsis of your story.

CHAPTER SIXTEEN

YOUR BREAKDOWN TEN QUESTIONS

*"I think the biggest mistake a lot of young,
newer writers make is they try to
write commercial movies.
They sort of figure, okay…
I'm going to write a Lethal Weapon because that did well,
or I'm going to write a cheesy horror movie.
They use that as the basis for what they write about
and how they write as opposed to saying
"Who am I as a person?
What do I have to say that's worth saying?"
Good writing is good writing because you feel something.
You have something important to say
and you have an interesting way of saying it,
not because you think you can do
what somebody else has already done."*

Michael Schulman
V.P. of Production for Summers-Quaid
Former Agent at ICM

*This exercise comes at a very precise moment of your script's development process: **The Breakdown**! We did earlier speak about breakdowns and how they are written…*

*A Breakdown is the most essential step before the actual script writing; it usually comes on the heels of a long, arduous and sometimes hopeless process through which you are finally able to garner four essential results: **Ideation, Synopsis, 5 P's, Characterization** and **Treatment**.*

*And I am not including your sleepless and tortured brainstorming nights! But it might be enlightening to remember how the experienced screenwriters look at this endeavor. Here for example is **William Link** who wrote and produced such successes as **Columbo, Murder She Wrote, Mannix, McCloud** and **Ellery Queen**, musing about this issue:*

*"**Many writers do not know how to tell a story. What they do is get a concept and sort of know what the ending is, but they don't have a clue how to get from that first scene to the climax. I think one of the major reasons for this is that most of the young writers don't read. That is a major, major problem. What they do is get all their input from TV or the big screen. I speak at universities all over the United States, and the young writers say to me: "How do I learn to write a mystery?" And I tell them to read the mysteries of the thirties. Read the Agatha Christies, the John Dickson Carrs, the Ellery Queens. They wrote rather bloodless characters, but their structures were impeccable. Their surprises were wonderful. Their ingenuity was first-rate. You really don't get that anymore."***

*   **John Schimmel**, a story editor at **Warner Brothers**, calls for other qualities in a script: "**Originality of vision is important. The things that are getting bought here have, by and large, a really unique voice or point of view — an entirely original take on its subject matter.**"*

The following ten questions will help you to better assess your breakdown, once written; how is it working, or not, and how exciting your story is likely to be.

Again, don't force yourself to answer every single question. If you can't, there is a problem! Review that question or aspect, rewrite, recreate, change, scrap, add, subtract, whatever…

But at least you know where the problem is!

1/

How do you introduce your protagonist and antagonist?
Do we see each in a way that is expressive,
attractive, likeable, offensive, evil, horrifying?
Is it visual? Does your introduction help set the tone
of the characters?
How about secondary characters? Do you give them
introductions too?

2/

Did you vary the time and place of your scenes in your
breakdown sufficiently?

3/

What is the purpose of each particular scene?
Why is it there, in that particular place?

4/

Does each scene advance the story, if it does?
Does it give any information about the story otherwise
difficult to obtain?

5/

Does each scene reveal something important about the
main character?
Does it set the tone or help the mood of the story?
Are any of your scenes static?

6/

"Whose scene" is each scene of your script? What do
they want in each? What are their obstacles to getting
it?
What is the conflict in each scene? Does it relate to
the main conflict of the story?

7/

What is the feeling at the end of your story?
How will the audience feel when they leave the
theater?
What about the Catharsis! Obviously, you should know
this before you start the script!

8/

Film loves contrasts!
Night/day, Interior/exterior, Action scene/Peaceful
scene. Night/Day. A claustrophobic scene in a jail
cell will definitely have more impact if followed by a
quiet scene, on a mountain lake.
Did you use contrasts in your script?
Read your breakdown again, scene after scene…
Are any of your scenes too similar to the one just
before it? Is it redundant? Does it take place again
in another room, in another office or street where
people just talk?
Think of other possibilities, places and scenarios.
Use contrasts!

9/

Scenes of preparation and aftermath usually take place
before or after essential scenes of conflict in the
script, when we are literally in the shoes of the main
character. We are drawn into her mindset. We know what
she is facing or just faced, and we understand what
she is thinking. Mood, music, sounds, props and
specific actions are usually vital in these scenes.
They give the viewers a chance to catch their breath
and do a little thinking and feeling!
Do you have any scenes of preparation and aftermath?
Are there moments when we really get to know the
character, when we are alone with her?
*Think of **Travis Bickle**, arming himself **in Taxi Driver**,*
just before the big action.

10/

Now think about your story structure!
Could you pinpoint your important script turning
points, twists, reversals, plot points and acts?

Act I:
Did you introduce properly, visually and attractively,
all the characters within their routine?
How about your break of the routine/inciting incident?
Did you make your hero face the new predicament? Did
you place her in the shoes of the proverbial
"reluctant hero?"

Plot Point I:
When are we clear that the character has to make a decision to pursue what he wants?
How do we know that? Can you make it clearer?

Act II:
Your character is now definitely drawn into the fight.
Did you put enough obstacles in her path? Are these obstacles truly unexpected and difficult, or rather, clichéd and contrived?
Are you making it hard, or rather easy for the characters to reach their goal?
Can you think of better obstacles?

Mid-Point:
This is a fundamental twist showing a surprising change of alliance between your main character and some of the major characters surrounding him.
Who turns their back surprisingly against him? Who against all odds takes his side?
How does he feel about it? Does he change his course of action? How does he pursue his goal from here on?
What does he learn from the experience?

Plot Point II:
Is there a low point?
Does your character reach her goal? What surprisingly happens when she does, or does not? Does she lose it again? Does she change her goal?
Do we see her commit to what she wanted again, with a renewed energy, despite the odds?

Act III:
What is the final obstacle, the final effort? Is it the biggest? What's at stake?
When is your climax?
Did your character really change? Is he really different than he was at the start of the story?
How do we visually see that change?
How does that help him reach his ultimate goal, or choose some other resolution?
How about catharsis?

CHAPTER SEVENTEEN

GET SMART

OR

THE NINETY-NINE SURVIVAL QUESTIONS

TO ANALYZING YOUR FEATURE-LENGTH SCRIPT

*"No matter what the genre — no matter how broad —
who the characters are, what they go through and
how they change is, to me,
what brings a screenplay to life.
No matter what kind of movie you are making,
I think it's best to think first in terms of the
character. In Lethal Weapon, it's not just bang-bang,
shoot'em up, but it's about a guy who really wants to
kill himself at the beginning because he's lost
everything and finds a reason to live at the end."*

Jason Hoffs,
Amblin V.P. of Development
(Steven Spielberg's company at Universal)

*I love that bumbling, awkward and clumsy **Agent Maxwell Smart.** But he wouldn't amount to much without **Ninety-Nine…***

*This exercise comes once you have achieved any draft of your script, but particularly what is known in the business as your **first draft**: you have finally put on the page all the amazing ideas you have painstakingly accumulated during the last several months, if not years, you have gone through numerous rewrites and it seems that you cannot further improve your script!*

Definitely an exhilarating and awe-inspiring moment…

But you should realize that it is just the first step in a long journey yet to come.

It is a journey rigged with uncertainty, fear and the apprehension one faces in front of the insurmountable amount of work that still lies ahead if you plan on getting anyone interested in your script.

*You have just entered the world of **Rewriting.** As indicated several pages earlier, rewriting is the most crucial activity in screenwriting, generally requested by a studio, a production company or any other entity remotely interested in your opus. Someone who has suffered the process long enough, labeled screenwriting as simply **"the art of rewriting…"** Studios, networks and production companies love to unabashedly call it by a different name: **Script Development!** As if that script was not developed enough before they came on board…*

However we look at it: Screenwriting is indeed mostly rewriting!

*Here is how **Tom Schulman**, who wrote among others, **What About Bob?, Dead Poets Society** and **Honey, I Shrunk the Kids,** sees it: **"I don't necessarily believe in the three-act structure when actually first writing something. However, I do find it a useful diagnostic tool during the rewrite: to go back over your draft to see if and where anything might have gone wrong or become unclear."***

So, your first draft is nothing else but material for better subsequent drafts. It's when you have the whole story on paper that you are able to address the issues a script faces, make the needed changes, create new scenes, swap existing scenes, scrap some that suddenly do not make much sense anymore.

But for that, you need some sort of direction: A tool to uncover what is working and what is not in your current draft. You almost need Maxwell Smart, as hilarious and ineffective as he might be. But you mostly need Ninety-Nine, his clever partner and alter ego who always saves the day with her wit and basic logic…

*I can't remember who said this first and it certainly doesn't matter: **Screenwriting is the art of asking the right questions and answering them!***

Once again, absolutely right!

*That's how we create, that's how we plot, that's how we structure and that's how we make people laugh or cry: By asking the pertinent questions again and again, and trying to painstakingly answer them. It starts generally with **"What if?"** and continues ad nauseam with: **"What will happen next? What would the hero do? How could he survive? What does she feel? What's his next obstacle?"**…*

Comparatively, that's also how we assess our first, or any subsequent drafts requested by the powers that be.

*A few days after you have completed your first draft and relaxed a bit in some remote location, far away from your office and your computer, read your script again and try to answer the following **Ninety-Nine Questions** as frankly and candidly as possible.*

Frankly, most screenwriters are not smarter than Maxwell Smart at this point of their script. Most are uncertain, bumbling, clumsy, and definitely lost in the meanderings of their own story.

And they really need Ninety-Nine…

If genuinely and truly answered, the Ninety-Nine following questions should effectively help you pinpoint any weaknesses in your script, any elements that need review or rework and any uncertainty about your characters, plot, structure, the story you are telling and a whole slew of issues usually addressed in any respectable script.

So, Go Ahead, Get Smart!

Your Main Character

1/ Is it clear to the viewer who your main character is?

2/ Does he have a real drive and goal?

3/ What are her fears, uncertainties, doubts, suspicion and inhibitions?

3/ What are the passionate, cherished, secret desires, hopes and dreams of your main character?

4/ What does she want? But what does she really need? Is that need vague, undefined or uncertain?

5/ Is the hero too passive and reactive when faced with the dramatic circumstances? Does he ever make decisions?

6/ Is the main character unattractive, dull or boring?

7/ Does he have a clear point of view?

8/ Does she disappear off the page for what seems to be a long time?

9/ Is your hero too weak, overpowered by other characters?

10/ What is the worst thing that could and hopefully will happen to him?

11/ What is your character's dramatic arc? Is it too thin, too superficial or too vague?

12/ Does he ever grow through the story?

13/ Are her actions contrived and predictable?

14/ Is he a loner with no one to talk to? Why?

15/ Is there empathy or identification at any moment with her and her cause? What will the audience think of your main character?

16/ Does he really solve his problems, or are there other characters who end up doing it for him?

17/ Are you actually your main character?

Other Characters

18/ Do you have a worthy antagonist? Other than him, who are the characters that are a threat, who try to stop, ridicule or destroy your character's plans?

19/ How do they try to mislead, misdirect, confuse or outwit your main character? Through accusations, direct lies or insinuations? What tactics do they use, what mimicry, what subterfuge, what trap? What are the social reasons for their actions?

20/ Who are the people your main character can rely upon or hopes to get on his side? Why?

21/ How do they try to help, support, reinvigorate or energize your main character? What do they do when the hero needs them most?

22/ What are their secret reasons in helping the hero? Is it altruism, love, friendship, family ties, fear, money, pity, subordination, etc.? How do they mobilize their forces?

23/ Are their relationships vague, weak or ambiguous? Are they flat, one-dimensional or stereotyped? Are they too thin and do not reveal anything about themselves?

24/ Are they reactive or active?

25/ Are their actions contrived or predictable? Are they too chatty? Do they explain too much?

26/ Are there too many characters? Are they too internal, expository or shallow? Do they all sound the same?

27/ Are they paid off? How? If not, why?

28/ Do they have more dramatic impact than your hero?

29/ At what moment does your antagonist feel triumphant? How can you increase her determination not to give up, to not show restraint, and fight to the bitter end?

30/ What characters can act as catalysts so they could alter or increase the antagonist's or the protagonist's reactions?

Conflict

31/ What is the main conflict at play? Is it internal or external?

32/ Is there enough conflict? Why not?

33/ Is it expressed through dialogue or action?

34/ Are there enough scenes designed to externalize the internal conflict?

35/ Are there enough scenes designed to express the internal elements of an external conflict?

36/ Is what the hero tries to achieve difficult, but possible?

37/ Are there enough real and worthy obstacles?

38/ Are the emotional stakes high enough?

39/ Is there uncertainty? Do we have "hope vs. fear" situations?

Story and Plot

40/ Is the story material flat and boring?

41/ Do we have an objective or a subjective drama?

42/ Is the dramatic premise clear? What can you do to eliminate the audience's disbelief (suspension of disbelief…) in the initial situation?

43/ Does the story line seem unstructured, choppy, loose or disconnected?

44/ Does the story seem incoherent, overly plotted, confusing or complex?

45/ Is the story episodic, predictable, contrived or too expository?

46/ Is the story fuzzy and thin, without subtext or discernible theme?

47/ Does the story scatter around in too many directions or get bogged down in too many details? Is too much happening too fast without focus on the story line?

48/ Does the story lack tension and suspense? Are your story's events sufficiently important and impressionable?

49/ Is there a time frame, a deadline or ticking bomb for the action to come to a resolution? If not, could there be one at any moment?

50/ Do you explain the story points again and again?

51/ Does it seem there are actually two stories in one?

52/ Is there a process of emotional participation? Or is the viewer a simple witness of events he doesn't really care about?

Action

53/ Does the action move the story forward?

54/ Are some of the actions incomplete?

55/ Do we feel that something seems to be missing?

56/ Is the action moving nonstop? Is it monotonous, or does it build slowly, fast?

57/ Are the events contrived and predictable?

58/ Are all the incidents paid off? If not, why?

59/ Is too much or not enough information revealed?

Visuals

60/ Is the story revealed visually or is it rather told through lengthy lines of dialogue?

61/ Are all your actions visually conveyed? If not, why?

62/ Is the visual expression too static? Do you have enough internal motion within each of your pictures? Is there enough external motion planned through editing, pace and rhythm?

The Mood

63/ What is the prevailing mood of your story?

64/ How do we feel the rhythm of the story? Does the main action's pace accelerate, decelerate or stays hopelessly the same during the entire script?

65/ At what moments do you feel restless, angry, revolted, unhappy or unsatisfied as the events unfold? At what moments do you feel calm, comfortable, happy and satisfied?

Places And Spaces

66/ Do the chosen locations make the story and the scenes more dramatic, more complicated, more difficult and more revealing for the characters? If not, can you change some of them to make your scenes and your story more exciting?

67/ What are the places where your characters don't want to go or are afraid to go to? Did do you force them to go there? If not, Why?

Structure

68/ Is there a Break of the Routine? When is the audience hooked?

69/ Do you have the necessary plot points to sustain your story line? Do they come at the right time?

70/ Is there a climax? Does it come too early, too late?

71/ Do you have clear crisis, reversals and twists?

72/ Are there too many twists, turns and subplots?

73/ Is your script too long?

74/ Is your first act too long? Is your second Act too short, too long, too weak or too boring with too little happening?

75/ Is the third Act too short, with too many endings? Do you have a resolution?

Dialogue

76/ Is the dialogue too wordy, too direct, too specific, too vague or too melodramatic?

77/ Is it too literary, too flowery, too stilted, too obvious or too On-The-Nose?

78/ Is it dull, awkward or basically conversational?

79/ Is everything explained through dialogue?

80/ Do characters always agree when they talk together?

Scenes

81/ Are your scenes too long, too complicated, loaded with too many details, too many directions and a lot of futile explanations?

82/ Is there enough action within each scene?

83/ Are there plantings and payoffs in each scene?

84/ Do the scenes lack a purpose and a function?

85/ Are you getting into the scenes too early and exiting too late?

86/ Do you have elaboration scenes, elation scenes and ellipsis scenes? Have you included an obligatory scene and a scene of recognition?

87/ Are your scenes going on ad nauseam from interior to interior to interior or rather from exterior to exterior to exterior?

Ending

88/ What is the last thing the main character finds out? What hopes still remain for him?
89/ What are the most feared confrontations he vainly tried to avoid, postpone or deny? Does he end up facing them? If not, why?

90/ Is the resolution becoming inescapable?

91/ What does "victory" or "defeat," mean by the end of your story?

92/ Does the ending really work? Does it really express your initial premise?

93/ Is the story's resolution paid off?

94/ Does the ending seem too soft, unsatisfying, weak, confusing, contrived, redundant or predictable?

95/ Is there a surprising twist that comes out of nowhere? Or did you end up again with a "Deus Ex Machina" situation?

96/ Is the ending not big enough or not commercial?

97/ Or is it too big with potential budgetary problems?

98/ What are the viewers' feelings when the story ends?

99/ Is there a catharsis? Did you give the viewer something to leave with?

A FEW WORDS IN LIEU OF AN EPILOGUE

I do not like books,
I do not trust books,
I do not believe in books!

By now you know which books I really have in mind and this textbook was not meant to be one of them.

This textbook is not meant to replace neither the actual learning experience in class, nor the constant writing and rewriting of scenes, dialogue and scripts beyond the class. It just helps it!

This textbook supposes that you come to class with some sort of talent: an already ingrained desire to tell exciting stories, some sort of mature and inspiring life experience, the necessary discipline to sustain a continuum of creative endeavor and the ability to see your script through completion despite the suffering and the odds.

Talent, or imagination or creativity or whatever you want to call it, is mostly about seeing what other people fail to see. Talented people, creative people, artists are able to discern with a sort of sixth sense-like acuity problems unseen by others as well as their likely or unexpected solutions.

Talent is something you already have in you, in whatever quantity, while craft and technique are something you acquire, you learn, you experience, particularly in class and in the field.

Talent is the ability to see and imagine beyond your life experience, the ability to transcend those quirky ideas or observations and find ways how to transform them into exciting stories.

Talent helps you select the right material, the right ideas and the right connections between them in order to create the best possible story. However, technique and craft help you translate these ideas on the page, tell them, narrate them in the form of an attractive story.

In a nutshell, talent helps you create an exciting story about exciting characters; craft and technique help you narrate that exciting story in the most exciting way!

In class, you can learn the craft and the technique and you could become very good at it. But in terms of talent and creativity, all you can do in a class is learn how to improve, how to increase, how to ameliorate whatever amount of talent you bring in.

Again, read carefully: **Improve, increase, ameliorate…**

All of these verbs suppose that something is already there to… improve, increase or ameliorate. You can't improve something that's not there, just like you can't restore a house that didn't exist first, or ameliorate a kitchen that has never been built.

This textbook is offering you the very basics of the technique and very little craft. The talent will depend on what you bring to class!

Now you are ready to start the process of learning how to write a script. We have barely peeled the first layer of the onion, as they say… There are many more layers, a lot more tears and probably a lot more suffering and frustration.

Remember the dire predictions from **Sunset Boulevard: "You'll get rewritten even after you're dead."**

But remember also **Ernest Hemingway's** *famous advice:* **"The most essential gift for a good writer is a built-in, shock-proof shit detector."**

So, despite the suffering and frustration, there will be a lot of intense satisfaction and a lot of exhilaration as well! And as far as I am concerned, we all work for those rare moments of exhilaration and satisfaction, as few as they might be.

Guess what: It's worth it! So, keep writing!

ACKNOWLEDGMENTS

OK! This is my Oscar moment, my Academy Award speech.

And just like all winners promise, this will be short!

My gratitude goes first to my students. All of them!

The ones who graduated and continue writing; the ones who got burned and gave it up; the ones who just had to survive one or two required classes and got the hell out of screenwriting as soon as possible; the current ones who are putting up the good fight despite the odds; the future ones who have no clue what mess they are getting into.

They all participated, or will participate in this textbook by asking the pertinent questions, by insisting on getting answers that make sense, by challenging me and others to transcend the routine, the traditional, the common, the run-of-the-mill, the usual, the prevalent, the ordinary, the mean…

They intrigued me, they surprised me, they exhilarated me, they inspired me, they provoked me, they motivated me, they chastised me, they reminded me of undue complacency and comfort, and through their scripts they opened my eyes to screenwriting aspects it would have taken me years to uncover.

I am forever indebted to them, all of them!

My sincere appreciation and my deep thanks go next to my colleagues. All of them!

I cannot imagine being around a better bunch of dedicated teachers whose passion for film and knowledge of the craft is truly difficult to surpass.

Particularly Alan Miller, academic, author and my partner for more years than we both care to remember in screenwriting crime, and other crimes… But who's counting?

And Jeremy Bandow, my former student and current colleague who surpassed all our expectations and proved to be as excellent a teacher as he was a student and a writer! I love how the tables have turned, and here is Jeremy reviewing the book that he pretends helped him become who he is. At least, that's what he tells the world, but who really knows? Whatever the case may be, he had to survive the successive drafts of this irreverent textbook, and he is still apparently recovering. Thank you Jeremy for your feedback, your suggestions and you insightful comments.

My sincere thanks go to all the other friends and acquaintances who unwittingly and unknowingly became the unfortunate reviewers of this book! Thank you for your "careful" comments, your thoughtful notes, your expert eyes and your pertinent remarks.

Finally, my love to Hana, my wife who tolerated me and wisely realized that, the best way to help me was to leave me alone and, get me out into the fresh air from time to time, so that I don't… rot or… calcify in my office!

I would like to close these remarks with the sobering words of **Anthony Minghella**, who wrote the seminal **English Patient** and **Truly, Madly, Deeply**: **"In America, before they make a film, they always ask you: What shelf is the video going on?"**

I wonder on which shelf this book is going to land…

THE GLOSSARY

OR

A HUNDRED OR SO ESSENTIAL DEFINITIONS YOU CANNOT SURVIVE WITHOUT IN SCREENWRITING

"I find a new attitude now of 'who cares?'
It's mostly because the writers aren't clever or patient
enough to sit down and really work out their clues.
On Columbo we would sit down and maybe spend a week just
on one clue. Now writers don't want to do it.
It's too difficult for them.
When we brought Columbo back,
it was so hard to find writers because a good mystery is
so difficult to structure.
It's much easier to write a car chase show or one that's
full of sex, going from bed to bed.
That's easier for a writer.
You can make the money faster."

William Link
Writer/Producer
Columbo, Murder She Wrote
Mannix, McCloud, Ellery Queen

1/ Acts

This refers to the major dramatic units of a screenplay, consisting of a number of scenes and basically covering the beginning, middle and end of a story in the traditional three-act structure.

2/ Adaptation

The process of creating a screenplay based entirely, partially or loosely on any kind of existing literary material such as a stage play, a novel, a short story, a magazine article or even a newspaper story.

3/ Antagonist

Simply stated: The Protagonist's opponent.
It could be a person, an institution, a natural force, an environment, a mysterious power from the mystical or metaphysical realm or even one's self, fighting to prevent the protagonist from reaching his/her goal.

4/ Anticipation

Or **Suspense, Tension,** apprehension and fear for the well being of the main character expressed through the process of identification. In a sense, it is simply the viewer's reaction to the main character's predicament. It exudes an uncertain state of mind, an oscillation between hope and fear about the outcome of the hero's efforts.

5/ Arc

As in **Character's Arc,** or growth, development and hopefully a notable or radical change of the main character through the course of the story.

6/ Atmosphere

Or **Mood, Tone.** Otherwise, what do you actually feel when watching a movie or reading a script. Mood refers to that certain quality, that aura or emotional feeling created by the writer through a clever manipulation of tempo, visuals, descriptions and their pace, vocabulary, dialogue, sound, ambiances, the choice of sets, locations and times… Your script could feel gloomy, romantic, depressing, light, frivolous, dark, romantic, revolting, bitter, cynical, allegorical, satirical, etc.

======================

7/ *Background*

Or **Biography, Backstory!** It highlights any and all objectively and emotionally significant events in a character's life, before the start of the story.

-/ *Backstory*

See **Biography, Background.**

8/ *Beat*

Simply stated, a **Pause,** whether in dialogue or action. Actors and directors hate when writers use it, thus pretending to tell them how to act or how to direct… So, simply avoid it!

-/ *Biography*

See **Backstory, Background.**

9/ *Breakdown*

Erroneously confused with **Outline** or **Step Outline.** During the development phase of a screenplay, a breakdown is the shorthand, telegraphic presentation of the story's events, introducing the actions that take place in each scene of the script with a slug-line and a few sentences describing the action. It's a powerful brainstorming tool to assess the viability of your plotting and your resulting structure without having to write scenes that you might not even need later.

10/ *Break of the Routine*

Also known as **Inciting Incident, Point of Attack.** This is simply the event that sets the story into motion and launches the beginning of a situation that will later expand into a full-fledged conflict between the characters.

======================

========================

11/ Catastrophe

Or **Outcome, Denouement** and **Unknotting.** It is the decreasing action following a story's climax and the tying up of a script's loose ends through the final resolution. In other words, each character, situation and story element needs to be satisfactorily resolved by the very end of the script.

12/ Catharsis

The process viewers experience at the end of a movie; the opportunity to "purge" themselves of whatever painful, exhilarating, exuberant or euphoric emotional build up that occurred during the course of the movie. Don't ever end your script without a catharsis, as the viewer would feel intense frustration.

13/ Character, Characterization

All the real or fictitious people who, for whatever reason, participate in the events of a story. Characterization is the compilation of any and all details of physical appearance, personal behavior, professional experience and psychological complexity created by a screenwriter to define a particular character as a believable individual.

14/ Cliché

Or **"Clichéd."** Meaning a contrived, trite, corny, stale, On-The-Nose, stereotypical and generally worn-out expression, action, character, motivation or story development.

15/ Climax

Or **Culmination.** In a screenplay, this is the point at which the conflict between drive and danger reaches its ultimate peak. Otherwise considered to be the highest emotionally turning point in a movie, its final battlefield.

16/ Coincidence

*A dramatic situation in which events seem to happen by accident and without any logical reason but the writer's convenience. Coincidence is considered as a contrived, clichéd, or on-the-nose way to resolving dramatic conflicts, and usually leads to situations from the realm of what is known as **Deus Ex Machina**. See later further meanings!*

17/ Collision

The slow or sometimes sudden setup of a dramatic situation leading to the principal conflict in a story. It essentially signals the start of the main tension in your script. Usually in Act I.

18/ Complication

*Also known as **Crisis,** or an unanticipated story development that puts the main character in a new and unexpected situation where reaching his/her expressed or implied objective becomes questionable.*

19/ Conflict

Simply stated: Two forces in dramatic opposition. In a script, it is the fundamental interplay between two or more forces seeking to reach either the same exact goal, or mutually incompatible goals.

20/ Confrontation

A unit of conflict, obviously within a scene in which one character or group of characters attempts to reach an immediate goal and another character or group of characters attempts to prevent them from reaching that said goal.

21/ Contrivance

*Or **Gimmick, Formula, Trick, Device** and **Tool**. It is a clever plot device used to help resolve a particular dramatic problem in a script.*

22/ Contrived

*Also known as **On-The-Nose, Clichéd**. A label with a pejorative connotation, implying that a particular* *device or element of the script - dialogue, situation, action, mood, character behavior, etc. - feels or rings unbelievable, artificial, superficial, false and is primarily used for the writer's convenience. This is when, for instance, you put words in the mouth of your character in order to directly give the viewer some important information, yet the character doesn't dramatically need to say any of that.*

23/ Coverage

A quick report delivered by a professional reader to an executive, a producer or an agent following the reading of a submitted screenplay. Generally it contains a synopsis, a brief evaluation of the script quality and potential production values as well as a rating of the various elements such as: characters, dialogue, structure, story, plot, writing, etc.
*It also includes a final verdict in the form of two laconic words: The blissful **Consider**, if they like it, and the kiss of death: **Pass**, if they hate it.*

-/ Crisis

*See **Complication**.*

-/ Culmination

*See **Climax**.*

========================

-/ Denouement

*See **Outcome, Unknotting, Catastrophe**.*

24/ Descriptions

*Also known as **Directions** or **Stage directions**. These are the explanations describing a setting, location, situation, character, action, sound effect, ambiance, etc. They are used to help you convey the events of your story, present your characters, describe their actions and reactions, and generally set up the mood of your narration.*

**-/ Device**
    See **Gimmick, Contrivance, Formula, Trick** or **Tool**.

**25/ Deus Ex Machina**
    Literally, Greek for: **God From a Machine!** It simply means, when the Gods, (and in our case the gods are the screenwriter!) intervene to resolve a character, a situation or the whole outcome of a screenplay from a logical conclusion, evident and unavoidable to all viewers.
    This directly relates to situations that are: **Cliché, Contrived** and **On-The-Nose**.

**26/ Dialogue**
    Or **Dialog**. These are the words, any words spoken by characters or a narrator in a story.

**27/ Diegesis**
    This is the Greek word for "recounted story" or simply, storytelling. A film diegesis refers to the total world of the story's action and sounds.

**28/ Diegetic Sound**
    Or **Actual Sound** exists when the source of a particular sound is either clearly visible on screen or considered to be present through the introduced action. This could be the voice of the characters, the sounds made by objects on screen or in the scene, such as a radio or TV, or the music coming from instruments in the actual location. Diegetic sound can be either on screen or off screen depending on whether its source is within the actual scene or in its vicinity.

**29/ Directions**
    See **Stage Directions** or **Descriptions**.

**30/ Directing**
    Or **Mise-en-Scene**, which literally means directing in French. And a director in France is known as a **Metteur-en Scene**. Mise-en-Scene is the aesthetic interpretation of a script, its visual expression and its transcendental exegesis through the process of

lighting, blocking for the camera, composition, filming and mostly editing.

31/ Dissolve

*Or sometimes **Dissolve To:** This is a transition in which a picture smoothly replaces another through a soft superimposition. It generally conveys a time or a space transition.*

32/ Drama

A script, a film or a TV program in which a story is narrated visually through the actions and the dialogue of characters who are caught in the throes of a strong conflict where each side is struggling to reach their own stated or hidden goals.

33/ Dramatic Intent

This is basically the main question you ask or the thought you express in your script as well as your attempts to answer it through your story. In other words, dramatic intent ends up being the fundamental dramatic purpose of your script.

34/ Dramatic Irony

This is a very privileged situation in a story in which the viewer, through cleverly crafted events, happens to know more than the main character. It's a comforting feeling that translates into a heightened level of dramatic tension and emotional rooting for the well-being of the hero.

35/ Dramatization

The process of creating a screenplay based entirely, partially or loosely on real life facts or events or real characters, deceased or still alive.

=======================

36/ Elation

Or **Scene of Aftermath.** It is a scene where both the character and the viewer get the opportunity to emotionally digest the impact of an immediately preceding dramatic moment or scene.

37/ Elevator Pitch

Also known as **Teaser Pitch.** It is meant to be a very short pitch, no more than a few sentences, cleverly designed to hook the listener by way of quickly pitching them the unusual premise, the particular genre and the production potential of your story.

38/ Empathy

Literally, it is the awareness of the circumstances, personal experience and background that drives a viewer towards a better understanding of a character's motivations. The result is a rooted viewers' tendency to emotionally share the characters' predicament. They tense up if a threat jeopardizes the hero's well-being, and they relax when the hero overcomes a mortal danger.

39/ Episodic

A screenplay, generally a TV dramatic form, structured in a series of episodes intended for broadcast at regular times of the week or the day

40/ Establish (To)

Or **To Reveal,** to acquaint the viewers with any and all important elements that help them understand and appreciate a story, as well as its relationship to all other elements in the movie.

41/ Exposition

The preliminary introduction of information necessary to understand a film story: Who, what, when, where, why, under what circumstances.

42/ Externalize

The process by which a screenwriter reveals to the audience through actions what is actually happening inside the character. Usually, gestures, dialogue, *facial expressions or crafty symbolism could help in that sense.*

========================

43/ First Draft

The draft you turn in to a producer, even if it happens to be your personal draft number 75…

44/ Final Draft

*Also known as **Polish**, it is technically the ultimate draft of a script, the one that you, or someone else designated by the studio or the producer, revises as many times as humanly possible until ready for production.*

45/ Flashback

This is when you visually present, on screen, earlier events from the factual or emotional perspective of one of the characters in your story.

46/ Flashforward

This is when you visually express on screen future events, dreams, nightmares and visions predicted or imagined by your character.

47/ Foreshadowing

*Also known as **Planting**, or in Tinsel Town parlance, **Laying Pipe**. It's a seemingly offhand revelation of an idea, character, property, costume, set… to be cleverly and more significantly used, or paid off later in the film. It is generally used to build participation, anticipation and suspense.*

-/ Formula

*See **Trick, Device, Tool, Contrivance** and **Gimmick**.*

========================

====================

48/ Genre

A kind, a category, a group of movies or TV Programs that happen to share similar aesthetic, stylistic, thematic, emotional and structural elements as well as parallel outcome and resolution.

-/ Gimmick

*See **Formula, Trick, Device, Tool** and **Contrivance.***

====================

49/ Hook

A unique situation, an astonishing incident or an unusual action or aspect cleverly and dramatically used to attract the viewer's attention at the beginning of a script.

====================

50/ Identification

Literally, the process of perceiving someone else, the character in this case, as yourself! When all works well in a script, it is the emotional state the viewer reaches when they forget about their own existence and project themselves completely in the hero's persona. They become one with the hero, root for them, fear for them and cry when they suffer.
This is, in other words, a screenwriters' nirvana…

51/ Inciting Incident

*See **Break of the Routine** or **Point of Attack.***

-/ Impediment

See Obstacle.

==========================

52/Laying Pipe

See **Planting, Foreshadowing.**

53/ Logline

It is the one-line premise of your story. Never longer than one or two sentences! It basically encapsulates in an exciting way the substance of your story, the main character, the conflict and the very original concept and aspects that make your story so unique.

===========================

54/ Master Scene Format

A script written in the Master Scene Format details the action and dialogue, but does not include any shooting instructions, camera angles or shots. It is written in scenes, each led by a heading or slug such as: EXTERIOR or INTERIOR, PLACE, TIME OF THE DAY.

55/ McGuffin

In a script, that's the one **"thing"** the **"contrivance"** everyone is trying to get, save, steal, possess or get rid of… For example, the statue in The Maltese Falcon.

56/ Melodrama

A pejorative concept describing a highly emotional story, generally based on stereotypical characters, intense sentiments and emotions, lots of crying and an expanse of music to heighten the ultimate melodramatic outcome.

-/ Mise-en-Scene

Literally **Directing**, in French. And a director in France is known as a **Metteur-en Scene**. Mise-en-Scene is the aesthetic interpretation of a script, its visual expression and its transcendental exegesis through the process of lighting, blocking for the camera, composition, filming and mostly editing.

57/ Montage

Simply stated: French for **Editing**. However, it slowly evolved into a storytelling device where a compilation of short visual images from different locations and times introducing different actions executed by different people is used to create a particular idea or emotional effect: The passage of time, the gradual change of a given situation or the transformation of a character following some psychological upheaval.
All the shots of a particular montage are introduced and labeled as one scene.

-/ Mood

See **Atmosphere, Tone…**

58/ Motivation

It is simply the real or implied, but almost always logical reason for a character's action.

======================

59/ Non-Diegetic Sound

Or **Commentary Sound** refers to a sound whose source is not visible on the screen and not implied to be present in the action, such as a narrator's comments, sound effects that are nonexistent on screen or its vicinity but added for dramatic effect, or a musical score added for emotional effect. Non-diegetic sounds come from a source outside the story space.

60/ Notes

These are the reactions or creative feedback given to the writer by a studio executive, a producer or an agent to improve the script.

61/ Nutshell Synopsis

It is a much shorter version of a synopsis, usually not longer than three to five sentences, designed to quickly inform a reader about the basic content of your script.

========================

62/ Obstacle

Or **Impediment**. That is any action, intention, person, unexpected event or even a small detail that your hero faces. It could make it difficult and sometimes de facto could prevent your hero from reaching their stated or implied goal. An impediment/obstacle could ultimately force your hero to change, alter or give up their original plan of action.

63/ Off-Screen

Written as **(O.S)** or **(o.s.)**
This happens when a real voice or sound is heard on screen, but the person who speaks or the origin of the sound effect is actually not present in the scene itself. That sound or voice usually comes from a space contiguous to the location we see on screen.

-/ On-The-Nose (OTN)

See **Contrived, clichéd.**

64/ Option

Also known in legalese terms as **Option Agreement**.
When a studio, a network or an independent producer has a strong interest in your script, it can offer you an option, or simply it can "option" your script.
In practical terms it means that they commit to buying your script within a **certain amount of time** (usually 6, 12, 18 or 24 months,) for a **defined amount of money**, if certain conditions are met. They also offer you a minimum amount of money called **advance**, usually 10% of the final settlement.
In exchange, during that set period of time, they will own the exclusive rights to peddle your script around, try to secure the financing and attach a director or specific stars in order to create what is known as a **package**.
At the end of the set period of time, they could **cancel the agreement** (the paid advance is obviously yours,) **extend the period of exclusive rights** for few more months and with more payment (usually another 5%) or **exercise their option,** which means pay you the rest of the agreed amount of money and own the property indefinitely.

-/ Outcome

See **Denouement, Unknotting, Catastrophe.**

65/ Outline

Or **Step Outline!** It is essentially a **prose format** document that introduces a chronological list of the actions in your script with none to very little dialogue. Imagine it as a series of short paragraphs, each listing one particular scene, with perhaps, sometimes, a hint of dialogue.

66/ Obligatory Scene

Generally, it's the film's climatic confrontation. A clever screenwriter usually prepares it from the very beginning by progressively planting dramatic elements throughout the story.
This is the scene viewers have been expecting with dramatic trepidation since the beginning of the journey and they would be really mad if somehow you omitted it.
Note: If by chance your obligatory scene takes place at a different moment than the climax, it usually

signals a particular mood and outcome for the movie:
before the 2 leads to a happy ending, after the climax
suggests a doomed and tragic ending.

67/ One-String Character

This is a memorable character without a defined line
of action, serving exclusively within one specific
scene, rarely in more than two or three.

========================

68/ Pace

Very simply, it's the speed at which you actually
narrate your story. It takes into account how fast
your actions are, how quickly you reveal information
to the viewer, how often your scenes change as well as
their length.

-/ Pause

See **Beat**.

69/ Payoff

This is the rewarding and deserved result of a clever
planting. It makes for a significant use of what was
previously planted, increases the viewer's
participation and sometimes allows for poetic
metaphors.
Warning: If plants don't get paid off, your audience
will feel frustration and disappointed. You don't want
that to happen.

70/ Peripetry

Also known as **Twist, Reversal**. It is an unexpected,
yet believable change of course in the story's action,
caused either by the main character's change of mind,
the intrusion of dramatically new circumstances in the
scene or simply as a result of the antagonist's
actions.

-/ Planting

See **Foreshadowing, Laying Pipe.**

71/ Platform

Or **Routine.** Otherwise, the quiet, safe and predictable routine of your hero before an unexpected event alters it, known as the **Break of the Routine, the Inciting Incident** or **the Point of Attack.** It generally comprises elements of the hero's daily life, habits, points of views, hopes, dreams, struggles, fears and desires.

72/ Plot

In the course of developing a screenplay, this is the dramatic plan of action concocted by a writer in order to control and manipulate the viewers' emotions at any given moment of the story.

Note: I hate the word manipulate for its negative connotation… I personally prefer: Influence!

73/ Pitch

A brief and exciting summary of your story emphasizing its concept, genre, plot, major characters and unique narrative and visual qualities. This is meant to be a dynamic verbal presentation! A writer is expected to perform it live as many times as it takes in front of studio executives, producers, agents, actors, investors or anyone who could acquire the script for production.

You guessed it: It's a de facto Sales Pitch that most writers just hate. But just like taxes and death, it is virtually unavoidable in your career…

74/ Pinks

When a script is acquired and goes through rewrites, even as a shooting script, all drafts and all changes are usually printed on pages of different colors: Pink, blue, yellow, green, etc. They indicate at a glance each rewrite and how much a script has been actually reworked, altered or **"butchered"** as most screenwriters think.

Today, regardless of the color used, Tinsel Town considers all rewrites as "Pinks".

-/ Polish
>See **Final Draft**.

75/ Predicament
>A dramatic situation so distressing and so emotionally disturbing for the hero that he/she is motivated, actually compelled, to immediately take action in order to change the situation.

76/ Premise
>This refers to the basic idea that propels you to create a story, its essence, its substance. It generally starts with the hypothetical **"What if…"** and must necessarily end with the reason why you ultimately wanted to tell the viewer that particular story!

77/ Proposal
>In business terms, this is a statement of purpose for your proposed movie including several pertinent business elements such as: Concept, target audience, production parameters, financing, etc.

78/ Protagonist
>The hero, the main character that moves the story forward at any given time in a script. They generally plan, decide and act, striving to achieve a particular objective, while the antagonist attempts to prevent them from reaching it.

=========================

79/ Query
>As in **Query Letter!** This is basically a pitch in the form of a letter where you try to convince a studio, a star, a producer, an investor or an agent to actually consider reading your work and personally meet with

you to discuss a possible collaboration or acquisition of your script.

===========================

80/ *Raising Action*
This happens usually towards the end of your movie, when you increase the momentum of the actions in your story as you move closer to the main objective. In practical terms it means you quickly reveal more essential discoveries, you speed the subplots along and you use shorter scenes, in different locations at a faster tempo.

81/ *Reader*
*This is traditionally an entry-level position for screenwriting graduates who are hired to read, analyze and submit to the studio a document known as **Coverage**, assessing all submitted scripts for quality and potential production values.*

82/ *Release Form*
In order to protect themselves and prevent lawsuits for plagiarism, studios, production companies and agencies request, mostly from screenwriters who are not represented by agents, this stringent legal document, often revolting to beginners…

83/ *Resolution*
The very last moments in a movie following the climax. It's finally the time when the audience feels, with the characters, the impact of the final battle that led to your climax. Now you are able to witness your hero walk as a transformed person towards a new future. The resolution also brings a closure to all loose ends, all subplots and all characters in the movie.

-/ Reveal (To)
     See **to Establish**.

-/ Reversal
     See **Twist, Peripetry**.

-/ Routine
     See **Platform**.

84/ Rhythm
     Literally, a recurring theme or action! In a script, it's the progression and the regular recurrence of scenes, actions, dialogue, locations, times of the day, interiors and exteriors or music and sound effects for a lasting dramatic effect; otherwise, the mood of your story.

========================

-/ Scene of Aftermath
     See **Elation**.

85/ Scene of Disclosure
     Or **Scene of Revelation, Scene of Discovery**! This is a surprising, usually unanticipated scene in which the main character, actually any character, finds out what was previously a mystery. For a better emotional impact, the viewer has generally discovered it long before through dramatic irony.

-/ Scene of Discovery
     See **Scene of Revelation** and **Scene of Disclosure**.

86/ Scene of Preparation

This is usually a scene leading to a highly dramatic moment (collision, twist, confrontation, revelation, obligatory scene, culmination…) and emotionally preparing the viewer through a sophisticated use of atmosphere, directly or through gimmicks, tricks and other devices.

-/ Scene of Revelation

See **Scene of Discovery, Scene of Disclosure.**

87/ Script Doctor

It refers generally to a screenwriter who is hired by a producer or a studio to rewrite or revise all or parts of an existing screenplay. Despite the negative connotation and the lack of direct credit, this is a respected and very well paid job sought after by many established screenwriters.

88/ Secondary Character

Also known as **Subsidiary** or **Subordinate Character.** It is a character involved in the main action by pursuing his/her own objective in a subplot. This is what Hollywood calls **Supporting Character.**

89/ Sequence

A major unit of action consisting of a number of chronological scenes, united by an objective that is, or is not, reached at its end. A sequence is generally centered around one idea or event: Arrival, wedding, moving out, trial, job search, etc.

90/ Series of Shots

As opposed to **Montage**, a series of shots usually shows the same character doing different actions in different times and spaces, and even sometimes in completely different locations. The best example would be your hero at home, going through different actions, as she/he gets ready to leave for work.

91/ Shooting Script

Conceived exclusively by a director and based on a screenwriter's final draft, it presents the action of a movie shot by shot, suggests all special effects, details all needed technical specifications and serves as the definitive blueprint for the entire production. It is also when, and only when, each scene is numbered!

92/ Spec Script

As in **script speculation**… A screenwriter might decide to write a particular script without getting paid, on speculation that a producer will pay him/her if they like it. Usually a tough call, but beginners and writers who have never been produced have to start there, no matter how talented they think they are!

93/ Spectacle

As in **spectacular**… Because the emotional impact of a movie relies heavily on pictures, spectacle refers to the kind and the quality of the visuals you use in your story. These, if well chosen, not only help understand the story, but might also create a heightened range of emotions such as fright, shock, awe, despair, disbelief or arousal.

94/ Split Page Format

A format generally used in Europe. In the US, videos, commercials, audio-visual works and generally non-narrative programs are presented in this format.
On a page vertically divided, you indicate on the left hand side your directions, and on the right hand side the corresponding sounds or dialogue.

95/ Split Screen

The visual effects by which you place in various sections of your screen different shots of different people doing different actions. A phone conversation showing both characters on a split screen would be a good example.
Warning: Directors hate when screenwriters take directorial decisions…

96/ Spine
The character's main objective, drive, fear or desire, the real backbone of your script!

-/ Stage Directions
*See **Directions** or **Descriptions**.*

97/ Stakes
*In a story, it's simply what's at risk, what could go wrong for your hero; it's literally anything that your audience could worry about, anything that could make them dramatically participate, anything that could make them emotionally stay involved until the very final resolution. Otherwise known as the **hope versus fear** process.*

-/ Step Outline
*See **Outline**.*

98/ Story
The record of how a hero deals with a particular dramatic situation or, simply stated, the progression of a film's events based on a given plot.

99/ Story Analyst
*A pompous title for a very basic but important job we already introduced: the **Reader**.*

100/ Structure
This would need several pages of definition... For the moment, it's the framework of a script, the foundation, the way events and scenes are cleverly organized in a pattern that is ultimately meant to create a lasting and dramatically emotional effect on the viewer. Imagine it as the structural foundation of a building...

-/ Subordinate Character
*See **Subsidiary** and **Secondary characters**.*

101/ Subplot

Simply put, the small-story-within-the-big-story.
It generally involves subordinate or secondary characters and develops actions and events parallel to the main action, thematically related to it in the form of variation or counterpoint.

-/ Subsidiary Character

See **Secondary** and **Subordinate Character**.

102/ Subtext

In a well-written script, it indicates a hidden meaning underlying the dialogue, plot, a specific action or certain visuals. Usually invisible to the viewer on a superficial level, it is revealed through clever hints and innuendos.
As **Tom Lazarus**, writer of **Stigmata** says: **"Text is what you say, subtext is what you really mean."**

-/ Supporting Character

See **Subsidiary, Secondary ans Subordinate Character**.

-/ Suspense

See **Tension, Anticipation**.

103/ Suspension of disbelief

This happens generally in the beginning of a movie when, through clever conditioning and adequate convincing on the part of a talented writer, an audience is willing to suspend its disbelief when faced with otherwise extraordinary, fantastical or highly unbelievable situations.
The reason is usually because the audience wishes to emotionally participate and thoroughly enjoys the dramatic developments of the upcoming story.

104/ Synopsis

It's the brief outline of a proposed film's content that should never be longer than one page if you want anybody who's anybody to read it!

=======================

105/ *Tag Scene*

A short scene that takes usually place following a script's climax and resolution; a final cathartic punctuation, as it were.

106/ *Teaser*

Mostly in television, a very exciting event, in the first few minutes of a show, designed to attract the viewers' attention and hopefully prevent them from flipping to the next channel.

-/ *Teaser Pitch*

See **Elevator Pitch**.

-/ *Tension*

See **Anticipation, Suspense**.

107/ *Theme*

It would also take us several pages to go through this one as well. For the moment, let's suffice with the following: Theme is the latent, implicit, deeply rooted moral message or profoundly human issue a movie deals with, its underlying meaning. It's really the argument of your script. Some people in the industry refer to it as the… **Thought**.

108/ *Ticking Bomb*

Also known as **Time Frame**, this is a deadline, an end to an action the audience can anticipate. It's a device you could use to help the audience store up emotional energy by letting them know about it in advance; dramatically, it could also be the time of a crucial action to be completed. A bomb that is going to blow up in twenty-four hours. A character in danger of being killed before dawn, as the serial killer stated in his letter to the police.

109/ Time Clock

Otherwise, how long in real time does it take for your story to happen. In practical terms, it's the time you allot for your characters to reach or achieve their declared objective. It might be days, months, years or sometimes just few hours.

-/ Time Frame

See **Ticking Bomb.**

-/ Tone

See **Mood, Atmosphere.**

-/ Tool

See **Gimmick, Formula, Trick, Device** and **Contrivance.**

110/ Transition

Simply put, it is the connection, the bridge from one dramatic scene to another. Examples of transition are: DISSOLVE, FADE OUT, FADE TO BLACK, FREEZE FRAME, *etc.*

111/ Treatment

A semi-dramatized, present tense narrative prose, introducing the basic story structure in a script with dialogue indicated only indirectly. It is generally five to thirty pages long for a feature-length film.

-/ Trick

See **Gimmick, Device, Tool, Contrivance** and **Formula.**

-/ Twist

See **Reversal, Peripetry.**

========================

===================

-/ Unknotting
See **Denouement, Outcome, Catastrophe.**

===================

112/ Voice-Over
Or, the mechanical transmission of a voice, known and used mostly as (V.O.) or (v.o.). The person who speaks is physically neither on screen nor in the immediate vicinity of the scene. Their voice is usually coming from some sort of communication device such as a telephone, a P.A. system, a TV, an amplifier, an answering machine or a narrator's voice.
V.O.'s are also used when a character, actually visible on screen, shares his/her thoughts and impressions with the viewer, or thinks out loud…

===================

113/ WGA
*Or **The Writers Guild of America**. It is the union representing the professional screenwriters and setting through a **Minimum Basic Agreement (MBA)** the basic parameters regulating the writing profession, including rates, credits, rights, regulations and other financial implications.*

THE INDEX

OR

HOW YOU FIND YOUR WAY IN THE HOLLYWOOD JUNGLE

*"In an American Film Institute brochure,
it says the three most important elements of screenwriting
are story, characterization and structure.
Well, that's not true.
The four most important elements are
theme, story, characterization and structure.
You have to know in some way what you are about to do. Even
if that theme gets rerouted and ends up in subtext, somehow
there has to be some sense of why you are doing this other
than to make money or to meet girls."*

Paul Schrader
Screenwriter

- *A* -

- *B* -

- C -

- D -

- E -

- *F* -

- *M* -

- 𝒰 -

- 𝒱 -

- 𝒲 -

- Z -

- Numbers -

CPSIA information can be obtained
at www.ICGtesting.com
Printed in the USA
LVHW020536060722
722780LV00008B/370